RECOVERING REDEMPTION

A GOSPEL-SATURATED
PERSPECTIVE ON HOW TO CHANGE

MATT CHANDLER
AND MICHAEL SNETZER

PUBLISHING GROUP

NASHVILLE, TENNESSEE

Dedication

From Matt:

I'd like to dedicate this book to the hundreds of men and women at The Village Church who have been freed from their bondage to fear, shame, addictions, and moral religion. Watching you struggle well and find vitality in Christ has been a joy of mine and fuel for my continued pursuit of the redemption found only in Jesus Christ. As I say often, I love you more than you know.

From Michael:

I'd like to dedicate this book to all those who have tuned the gospel out, thinking it was not their style. Stay tuned.

Contents

Cover Versions

You do it all the time. A song comes on the radio, and after the first two notes, you've already switched the station. Before you've listened to even one word, you've decided it doesn't suit you. Not your style. Not your thing.

But then one day you hear it playing in the background somewhere, maybe on a restaurant patio or at the beach or streaming out of somebody's car for twenty seconds at a traffic stop, and you realize . . . hmm, it's better than you thought. Surprisingly, it kinda speaks to you. Especially that message in the lyric. Maybe there's more to this person's stuff than you've given them credit for. Up till now, you've always tuned it out. Wrong vibe, wrong genre. Nobody you know or hang around with is into that kind of music. But if you knew where it could take you, if you'd known what this songwriter was wanting you to see, just by hearing it sung . . . and then singing along . . .

That's the kind of song we're here to play for you.

It's not a new song, really—the song of redemption, the gospel. It's been around for years. But when the message meets you in the right place, at the right time, the meaning that's always lived there can suddenly start to spill all over you. Even if the song's not new to you at all, even if you've heard it sung so often by so many singers—enough times that some of its luster has been lost in the repetition—the textures and tight harmonies can still come out of the blue sometimes and stun you with its layers, its beauty.

So it can capture you.

Or it can *recapture* you.

Doesn't really matter which one.

Because either way, it can sing to you.

And either way, it can change you.

Sure enough, maybe the gospel was the soundtrack of your teens, perhaps even younger. You heard it played, you were drawn to the lyric, it captured your desires. Met you at a deep, special place. You identified. You jumped on it. You'll always remember the first time you heard it—you can picture where you were, what you were doing, who was there, how you were feeling—the first time you *really* heard it, when you truly stopped to notice what you loved about it so much.

Or maybe it took the appreciation of being an adult, or being a parent—or just finally growing out of what you thought you liked so much about all that head-banging stuff you used to listen to—before you realized there was something about the gospel that was real and timeless. It finally *got* to you. Changed your life.

And that's great.

But unless we're missing our guess, your life and the gospel probably haven't always felt in sync on a lot of days, in most of the years since. After the emotional scene with the trembling chin and the wadded-up Kleenexes, where you truly felt the weight of your own sin and the Spirit's conviction, you've had a hard time consistently enjoying and experiencing what God's supposedly done to remedy this self-defeating situation. Even on those repeat occasions when you've crashed and burned and resolved to do better, you've typically only been able, for a little while, to sit on your hands, trying to stay in control of yourself by rugged determination and brute sacrifice (which you sure hope God is noticing and adding to your score). But you'll admit, it's not exactly a feeling of freedom and victory. And anytime the wheels come off again, as they often do, it just feels like the same old condemnation as before.

Devastating that you can't crack the code on this thing, huh?

You were pretty sure that being a Christian was supposed to change you—and it has. Some. But man, there's still so much more that needs changing. Drastic things. Daily things. Changes in your habits, your routines, in your choices and decisions, changes to the stuff you just never stop hating about yourself, changes in what you do and don't do . . . and don't *ever want to do again!*

Changes in how you think, how you cope, how you ride out the guilt and shame when you've blown it again. How you shoot down those old trigger responses—the ones you can't seem to keep from reacting badly to, even after you keep telling yourself to be extra careful, knowing how predictably they set you off.

Changes in your closest relationships, changes in your work habits, changes that have just never happened for you before, the kind of changes that—if you can ever get it together—might finally start piling up, you think, rolling forward, fueling some fresh momentum for you, keeping you moving in the right direction.

But then—stop us if you've heard this one before . . .

You barely if ever change.

And come on, shouldn't you be more transformed by now?

This is around the point where, when what you've always thought or expected of God is no longer squaring with what you're feeling, that you start creating your *own* cover versions of the gospel, piecing together things you've heard and believed and experimented with—some from the past, some from the present. You lay down new tracks with a gospel feel but, sadly, not always a lot of gospel truth.

See if this one, for instance, sounds familiar . . .

It starts off strong. Bold. Confident. Driving. Jesus loves you, He died for you, He's forgiven you. Good. This is going somewhere. Love it.

But then it starts feeling forced. You're rushing the tempo. You're trying too hard. Instead of letting the music come to *you*, instead of just enjoying where it's taking you, thankful for the privilege of just being invited into the band . . . you're pressing. You're overthinking it, overanalyzing. You're hitting the right notes pretty much, but you've lost the essence, the wonder, the pure pleasure of just playing, of being together.

And before long, the whole thing has turned really unpleasant—dissatisfying—both to you and to everybody else who's watching and listening. You start to question why you put so much of yourself into this, just to end up feeling so frustrated and unhappy. Seems as though trying to be good is too much work for what it gets you. But then again, *not* trying to be good costs you a lot of the affirmation and reputation you like. Makes you feel even worse about yourself.

So you set out to do better—even if it kills you, even if it means playing your own part and other people's parts too. You'll work harder at making music than ever. But in the end, you only succeed at turning what was once a passion into a performance. Into a personal growth opportunity, a profit margin. Always chasing, always making plans for improving. And yet it never feels good enough. Because *you're* never good enough. It never becomes as musical as you want it to, the way you always thought it would.

You could call this cover version the *uncovered* version— where whatever God did to convince you that He loved you and delighted in you, that He enthusiastically forgave your sins and welcomed you into His family, He'll never persuade you now that you don't need to be earning it. That's why you're trying so hard, isn't it? To keep Him happy with you? To score points with Him? To cover what His grace didn't catch the first time? And still, even with all of that, you can't seem to do it, can't seem to make the payments on your approval policy.

But that's not the gospel. Never has been.

Neither is this . . .

The one where your life just falls completely flat. You've lost your edge, lost your place. You're doing things good Christians don't do—things that often *you* don't want to do, even though you keep doing them, running back to them. So which is it? Is this the way you want it, or not? Hard to tell. You jump back into the chorus sometimes, hang tough there for a little while, but then you catch yourself pulling out your old music books again, going off-chart, drifting off-key.

You're a mess. You hate this. It's pitiful. You've taken your second chance (third chance, fourth chance, four hundredth chance) and fouled it all up, again and again. God may have been willing to save you on the front end, before He really got to know you. But after the kind of performance you've been putting up lately . . .

I mean, if anybody in your church and your family knew what you were really like underneath . . .

How could God love such a terrible singer?

Call this the fear of being *discovered* version—where you put your faith in a God who rescues lost people from their sins, but once those lost people become *His* people (and once they do the sorts of things you've done), He may or may not have a lot of rescuing left.

And that's not the gospel either.

Same goes for the ever-popular *undercover* version, where Christianity is seen only as a private thing, a personal conviction, something you might occasionally play through your speakers at home or through your earbuds while you're jogging, but never in public, never where people could see.

There are other versions too—*lots* of others—variations on the same theme. They feel like how we think God would feel, if we were God. They sound like what we hear in our heads sometimes, as if we can trust ourselves to know more truth than He knows, to be a better interpreter of His Word than He is.

If you've been singing and believing these kind of counterfeits, these cheap knockoffs—and trust us, there aren't many people who don't or who haven't—then a fresh cover treatment of the gospel might be just what you need to hear. It's what we all need to hear, repeatedly.

The sovereign love of God—bigger than us, bigger than everything.

Our utter incapacity to change ourselves—not before, not now, not ever.

The confidence of knowing full well we've been restored in Christ, while experiencing His active work of restoration day by day.

Living as children, not as slaves.

Growing in grace, not to get all A's.

We're praying for many blessings on your life as we go along, praying for a new brand of joy and freedom you've just never experienced before. Full acceptance in Jesus. A renewed desire for serving Him. Ongoing forgiveness for inevitably fallen people.

And change. Real change.

That's what comes from *Recovering Redemption*.

Again, we can't know what your own interaction with the gospel has been like so far. Maybe, quite honestly, you've just never believed it. You're intrigued enough to look into it a little bit, but you still don't see what people think is so great about it. It's just another song, like a lot of religious songs. Nice in small doses, but kind of pitchy in spots. Sort of dated. Maybe someday you'll learn to like it, but you've never been too impressed by it yet—nor by the people who go around singing it all the time. (Especially them.)

We just want you to know, this book is still for you. Whatever your reason for coming, it's really cool that God brought you here. Whether you know and can vividly recall how He's reached out to you in grace, though you've admittedly been far from perfect in living out your faith . . . or whether you remain very uncertain at this moment, skeptical even, about this whole Bible and gospel thing . . . there is much to ponder together here, opening our hearts to see in plain view not only the tragedies of our sin, but in all its beauty, the glories of His redeeming grace.

For some, refreshing.

For some, revealing.

For all, redemption.

Chapter I

Good. Gone. Bad.

Genesis, Creation, and Fall

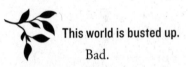 This world is busted up.
Bad.

Ask a parole officer. Ask a social worker. Ask a foster parent. Ask an oncology specialist. Some people's jobs keep them so far out there on the front lines, they see what's messed up about our society and human existence nearly every day. They see sexual predators soliciting nine-year-olds on the Internet. They see teenagers slicing thin lines into the skin on their inner forearms. They see bruises and broken marriages. They hear from a whole bunch of bald-faced liars. Blood and guts and death and disease. It's awful.

And in case you're not around a lot of people in professions like those, just ask a pastor—because outside of police officers, firefighters, and paramedics, we're often the first ones on the scene at emergencies and other moments of personal loss. We've been inside homes where the grief is so intense, where the pain is so hot to the touch, all a person can really do is just sit there and hold people, cry with them, wait it out. We've seen and (in Michael's case) personally experienced the dark realities of meth addictions, car crashes, jail cells—all kinds of lifestyle junk and near-death experiences. We've counseled with guys who've lost work, with teens who've lost their virginity, with families who've lost nearly every penny they ever had, even with people who seriously don't know where their next meal is coming from or where they'll be spending the night tonight.

How much time you got? We could go on all day.

And when it's not falling apart in front of *some* of us, it's falling apart in front of *all* of us—another school shooting, a missing child, another swath of tornado destruction, or a terrorist strike. If we're a safe enough distance away, we tend to move on in a day or two, once the CNN crews pack up from their remotes and leave the disaster site. But every time it hits again—and it always does, it always will—we're reminded just how close the next waves of sadness and despair really are. They're never much further away than a breaking news flash, a phone call, or a phantom pain in our side.

Sometimes, though, it's not the unexpected and extreme that show us how broken this world is, but more of what we might describe as a low-grade gnawing, deep in our gut, an inability to ever be totally satisfied by any event or experience that happens to us. Weekends and vacations are great—but never quite long enough. Live music concerts are big fun, take us to a whole other place—but then they're over, moving on to the next show in the next city. Fourth-quarter comebacks are crazy exciting. Cheers, jumps, and fist-bumps. But then the stadium clears out, the announcers sign off, and by the end of the day, we're home packing our sandwich and apple for work tomorrow.

So even if you're the kind of person who constantly keeps the glass half-full of optimism, there's still a limit on how high you can raise the water line of expectation—not and keep living in reality.

Our days will always be dammed up somewhat by the limitations of our own energy, by random intrusions of difficulty and conflict. We'll be forced to deal with unwanted obligations, with holdover consequences from past mistakes, with imbalances in our weekly schedules. We'll never be able to clear the harbor of every spiritual battleship threatening to take us down and blow us out of the water. And though we try not to look, we cannot keep the drug needles and dead bodies from washing up on shore every day with the morning headlines, even if we plug our ears with the squealing sounds of our preschoolers' play dates and our iPod playlists.

What's even *more* upsetting and discouraging is that we will pollute things even further with our own putrid mess of sins and habits, some of which we've allowed to bob along in the surf around us for years and years. Sure, we've tried dredging the lake from time to time, utterly disgusted with ourselves, doing our best to clean out what we've allowed to embed underneath. But the fresh water never seems to stay fresh for very long. We'll foul it up with something, if not with something else.

Bottom line, when we're not living in constant danger, seems like we're dealing with consistent disappointment—in ourselves, in others, or just in general.

And surely, we think, it doesn't have to be this way.

Surely there's more to life than this.

All right, let's hold it here, because what we want you to see in that very statement—in that feeling—is how this desire in your mind for something more and better is not the depressed ramblings of a bad mood, but is truly a God-wrought invention. It comes straight from your Creator. This discouraging take on things is in reality a gift from the One who made you. You can try dulling it with sleeping pills and police dramas if you want, but you'll be stamping out a fire that's actually *supposed* to be burning inside you. Because if you're looking at this world—and at yourself—and you're convinced that neither one of them is the way they're supposed to be, then you're being given an important piece of bad news.

And here's why you need to pay attention to it.

In order for good news to be good—like the gospel is good (literally means "good news")—it must invade bad spaces. When you receive a clean test result, for example, from a panel of lab work your doctor ordered, that's some *good news,* isn't it?—even better if you'd been preparing yourself for possibly the worst. When you ask someone to marry you, and they say "Yes, yes, I want to spend my whole life with you," that's *good news* too—because the alternative answer sure would've made for one nasty rest of the weekend.

The bad parts of what we see and feel around us serve a purpose in God's mission to recreate something that's been lost and destroyed. They keep reminding us of realities we'd just as soon forget, yet He uses them as goads to lead us toward an even fuller universe of truth.

Bad news is the backdrop against which good news really shines.

So let there be darkness.

And let there be light.

In the Beginning

Genesis 1.

God created.

And it was good.

The triune God of the universe—Father, Son, and Spirit—existing forever in perfect contentment with one another, overflowed with love and affection onto the canvas of creation, and brought into existence everything that's ever been.

They didn't *need* to. Didn't need you. God wasn't bored out of His mind or wondering what He wouldn't give if He could only find somebody new to talk to and hang around with. Wasn't that at all. On the contrary, the magnificent Three in One, in celebration of their fullness and perfect fellowship, delighted Himself/Themselves by speaking the powerful words that accomplished the creation of all things.

And it was . . . good.

What an understatement.

The act of Creation itself reads in the original language of the Old Testament with a pulsating cadence, almost like a musical rhythm: God created, God created, God created, it was good. A beautiful harmony, reflecting perfect union within the Trinity, became interlaced throughout star systems and soil samples, from the most mammoth and mountainous things to the most microscopic and mysterious things, congealing into a cosmos that was spectacular not only by its size and beauty, its grand colors and shared cohesion, but also by a tangible quality that noticeably pervaded it.

Peace.

His world was at perfect peace.

And then into the musical score of Creation, He inserted a well-timed rest. An intentional pause. Not *stopping* the music, but accentuating by silence the beauty of what was playing, putting space between the notes and bringing clarity to the whole work.

Perfect peace. Perfect harmony.

Try to imagine it. Here. On this blue planet. The same one where perhaps you kick off your shoes after work and peel open a lonely can of ravioli and a Diet Pepsi for dinner. The one where you wake up stiff from a cross-training routine, feeling older than ever, moaning yourself out of bed with whatever's grown knotted up in a ball overnight. The one where sexual lusts can sail through your head when you swear you were just stopping to fill up your tank at the gas station. The one where your kids need braces *and* glasses in the same year—the same year your company stops giving cost-of-living raises due to budget cuts.

"Surely it doesn't have to be this way. Surely there's more to life than this." Yeah, no kidding. But know this: there was a time when the first man and woman never contemplated such an abstraction. Nothing in their world was dead or dying around them. Nothing was ominous or unsafe. Nothing was leaking or running late or costing too much or hard to do. God was perfect, creation was perfect, they were perfect, *everything* was perfect. And life was just there to be lived within the unbroken freedom and shame-free fellowship that existed between mankind and God. What else? Why not?

That's how it was. That's how He created it.

The original man and woman needed God, yes. But not because they were fallen and sinful. They needed Him simply because they were human. He created us from the very beginning to live in a loving, dependent relationship with Him.

Got it? That was the plan.

A lot of times, when we start thinking about God and redemption—especially as believers who continue experiencing trouble with ourselves—we focus on our conscience-dragging depravity, the things in us that need change and recovery. We concentrate on how sinful we are. Which is true. "The heart is deceitful above all things, and desperately sick," the Bible says (Jer. 17:9). You won't hear us dodging that doctrine for one second. We're born bad. But only in proper context can this key bit of biblical theology be considered "foundational" . . . because man wasn't depraved and depleted at the beginning. Sin wasn't there, even on Day Seven. The Word of God begins where our understanding of the gospel needs to begin: amid the flawless glories of Creation.

Sky. Sea. Air. Water. Seed. Plants. Garden. Food. Birds. Animals. Beauty. Trust. God. Man.

Peace.

Whenever we feel the absence of peace—whenever our unmet longing for joy expresses itself as anxiety, or depression, or fear, or anger, or enslavement to any number of defeating sin patterns or addictions—the emptiness we're feeling and trying to fill is for what our relationship with God, by His loving choice, was always meant to be. Our angst comes from the underlying implications of Ecclesiastes 3:11, where the Scripture says God "has put eternity into man's heart."

Our souls, in other words, possess a dim memory of Genesis 1 and 2. And we miss it. We crave it. We need it. The desire for relating in authentic Garden of Eden transparency and openness with God is what causes such dark shadows of disappointment to lengthen behind everything else we touch, taste, attempt, and take on, in desperate attempts to try getting it back.

What we "groan" for, whether we realize it or not—along with all the rest of our now fallen world—is for the Genesis ideal, the "revealing of the sons of God," living in peace, perfection, and pure harmony with our Creator (Rom. 8:19). We want Creation restored. We want life to be what we know it can be . . . and we want it yesterday. That's where the nagging dissatisfaction of our heart comes from. We're not what we *should* be. We're not what we *long* to be. We're not what mankind truly *was* in the beginning with God.

But "in the beginning" is where we need to start . . . because we'll always find it hard to understand our dysfunction unless we understand what it means to function. We won't be able to make sense of our chaos and disorders without seeing what true order with God really looks like. We can never grasp the extent of our depravity until we recognize the excellencies of our created dignity.

And this is what God has chosen to redeem for us.

Through His grace.

Through the gospel.

So just sit there for a second. And look at it. Realize, from revisiting Genesis 1, that God has already shown us how He can take what is formless, dark, and empty—which, perhaps, is exactly the way you feel right now—and breathe His precious life into the most lifeless of situations. Making it . . . good.

Not by enrolling us in a program. Not by pinning us down, cold turkey. Not by impersonally, insensitively telling us to clean up our act—to think better thoughts, to choose better behaviors, to channel better emotions, to tap into the better angels of our nature. He does it simply by an act of His loving will, by introducing us to the relationship we need with Him.

Empowering us to make changes. Today.

For what's broken in us—what's aching for recovery—is beyond our ability to fix. And from the moment it broke, all attempts to redeem it by ourselves are doomed to futility and failure. *We need God.* Or else. Not just once. Not just to get His signature on our heavenly hall pass. But forever.

We will never get over needing Him.

For everything.

Breaking Bad

So, behold, it was good. Very good.

And then it broke bad. Very bad.

Genesis 1 and 2, meet Genesis 3.

> They heard the sound of the LORD God walking in the garden in the cool of the day, and the man and his wife hid themselves from the presence of the LORD God among the trees of the garden. (Gen. 3:8)

There's probably not a more heartbreaking verse in all of Scripture.

(Read it again, in case you skimmed over it.)

Adam and Eve had been placed within the pristine wonders of Eden, invited by God's design into a life of no shame, no hiding, no fear, no secrets, no need for sneaking around, nothing at all to worry about. They'd been given pleasant work to do. They'd been given each other, without so much as a stitch of clothes between them. And they'd been given an abundance of food options to choose from, with only one, single, very distinct exclusion—the one tree whose fruit, if they ate of it, could be counted on to kill them.

That was it.

And by observing that one clear-cut rule, within the bounty of blessing that was teeming all around them, they were set up perfectly for a life of blissful unity, along with the effervescent joy that was intended to flow from their being obedient to God. "Take off. Have fun."

But that tree—that one prohibited tree—kept looking better and more desirable to them than all the others put together.

We're pretty sure you know the story. The Serpent (Satan) slipped a line to the woman: "Are you sure God said you couldn't eat from any of these trees?"

"No, just not from *that* one. We can't even touch it, or we might die."

"Aw, come on, that's not true. He just knows, if you can get the knowledge that comes from that tree, you'll make a better god than *He* is. He's holding out on you, girl."

Adam, by this time, had come bumbling over from . . . who knows, naming another animal or something, wanting to check out what was going down in this other part of the garden for a while. And instead of stepping in to protect his wife from an obvious liar and intruder, instead of jumping on that snake with whatever came closest to looking like a shovel blade from his tool-shed, he just stood by while she sank her teeth into the first sweet taste of destruction. Then, not wanting to appear unsupportive apparently, he shrugged his shoulders, went along, and dug in too.

Whoa.

The next sound you hear in the Garden of Eden is the heaving, lurching, ear-splitting shatter of *shalom*, of God's peace, screeching violently out of phase with the pitch-perfect rhythm and harmony of His original creation. Outright rebellion had been declared against the King of glory. And suddenly, these experiences we know all too well now ourselves—guilt, regret, panic, disbelief, nervousness, blame, self-hatred, hypocrisy—all came shuddering through Adam and Eve's bloodstreams for the first time in their lives. Like ice water. And both of them ran. And hid. And hoped to God they'd somehow gotten away with it.

And so began our historical obsession with finding and sewing fig leaves. With dressing up our disobedience and hoping nobody notices. With doing whatever we can think of to remember that song we can almost still hear in our heads but can never quite seem to pull it out of our long-term memory.

Sin fractured the proper ordering of God's creation. It changed this place where we live. The Bible sort of boils down the damage report into two broad categories: *futility* and *pain*.

Futility. Paul said creation was "subjected to futility" (Rom. 8:20). That word conveys the idea of being hard-pressed, shoved down, confined, restricted. What had once been full and unlimited, easy as falling off a log, has now been turned into nothing but strain and struggle. Everything's an effort, just to get through the day, the week, the month. It's heavy. It's cramped. We're constantly bumping our head and our elbows against it. Projects that feel like they shouldn't take more than a couple of hours to do, they somehow end up taking a day and a half and three trips to Home Depot, looking for a new part on the shelf that resembles this one we broke and brought from home. The span of our life "is but toil and trouble," Moses said (Ps. 90:10). It's futile. Hard-pressed. And as if that's not bad enough . . .

Pain. More specifically, the Bible refers to it as the particular pain of "childbirth" (Rom. 8:22). Now obviously we as guys can't relate entirely to this experience, as perhaps you can. But the two of us have each been in the room when it's happened and have seen it with our own eyes. So you'll get no upstage comparison argument from us. *It looks awful.* Way worse than anything we've ever felt ourselves. If you're a mom who's carried around a little person in your belly for nine months, if you've breathed and pushed and screamed and sweated and wondered what's become of the juice in that epidural drip—hear it straight: mad respect from the two of us. We'll never be able to make this up to you. But as you think of it—the pain of childbearing, of childbirth—realize it's a direct result of what sin has done to our world. It's reflective of the pain that accompanies so many aspects of all our lives. And begin to understand, perhaps from your own personal exposure to it—*this is serious.*

We know, from reading on into the fallout of Genesis 3, the hits just keep on coming. Relational chaos. Work difficulties. And, of course, the granddaddy of them all:

Death.

"For you are dust, and to dust you shall return" (Gen. 3:19).

In keeping with the tone-deaf dysfunction of a fallen creation, the reign of death is now always out there for us, forming up into at least one little storm cloud even in the bluest sky on the clearest day. For what Adam and Eve began, we ourselves have continued—and can't help continuing—"All have sinned and fall short of the glory of God" (Rom. 3:23). We've joined them in rebellion. Willingly. Gladly. Therefore, we draw our checks from the same payroll department: "the wages of sin is death" (Rom. 6:23).

And this, of course, is bad news.

But into these bad spaces of pain and futility, of troubled relationships, difficulty, and certain death, gleams the only sure hope that counteracts each one of them with present-day, joyful perseverance and one-of-these-days paradise. Restored. The wolf lying down with the lamb. The lion chewing grass like the oxen. The deserts blooming with roses. The mountaintops producing sweet wine.

Till then, the longing of the God-created human soul causes us to recognize lack and want it gone, to experience peace and want it to last. But only the power of the gospel can meet us in a world currently deprived of so much that we desire, and redeem for us what God Himself has provided for our lives. For His glory.

Broken Pieces

Nina was at home with her four children—none of them older than five, one of them only a month old—when her husband called, late in the afternoon, telling her not to plan on him for dinner, that he wouldn't be there.

"Well, how late are you going to be?"

"No, I mean I'm not coming home."

"You're not coming home . . . tonight?"

"No, Nina. I'm not coming home . . . ever."

Talk about the world suddenly not being right. Shattered peace. Busted harmony. That's not to say their ten years of marriage had been Ken-and-Barbie perfect. It had grown increasingly difficult in spots, peppered with hurt and disagreement, but never to the point where she'd seriously contemplated four kids, no husband, no marriage, no backup, no relief from what those days can do to a mom, even in the best of situations.

And yet that's what was left for Nina to deal with. A messed-up life in a messed-up world. And it was now up to her to fix it. There wasn't anybody else to turn to.

Sure, God was there. He'd saved her as a twenty-year-old rebel. She'd done her best to keep Him placated by her good life, good church-going, good parenting—but, good Lord, there was only so much she could do. And now she was being forced to do it with twice the responsibility and half the stamina.

But you do it for your kids, right? You can't quit. Not on *them*. So you learn to live with the betrayal, the fatigue, the challenges, the self-pity, the long nights, the awkward conversations, the embarrassing questions. All of it. And you try to make it match up with your Christianity—which makes "Christianity" just something else to add to your already overblown to-do list.

And for Nina, it as quickly becoming too much "to do."

She sat in a crowded worship service one evening, bravely battling back against the stresses of her life by singing promises she wasn't sure she could believe, much less hope to expect or deserve. Her husband had let her down, life had let her down, God had let her down. Everything was impossibly wrong, completely out of tune. And in the midst of feeling herself coming totally unglued that night, fumbling nervously with a paper envelope that had been lying in the seat next to her, she started to fold it, and crease it, and (for whatever reason) tear it in half.

"Tear it more," the Lord seemed to urge her. "Tear it into pieces."

This wasn't how she usually interacted with God. She was in church here, okay? Couldn't be doing something destructive and distracting, something she'd fuss at her three-year-old for doing. But whether through obedient response to what she was hearing from Him in her spirit, or because of the sheer agitation convulsing in her heart, she quietly began bending that envelope over and over on itself—into quarters, into eights, into sixteenths—slowly curling away thin slivers of paper, then tearing them into even tinier shreds. Dozens of them, hundreds of them.

"Now put it back together," she sensed Him saying.

"It won't *go* back together."

"But that's what you're trying to do, Nina. Isn't it? You're trying to put yourself and your life, your world back together. And it's not going to happen. Not without Me."

She held what was left of that original envelope, now about the size of a dandelion puff in her hand, recognizing in that little clump of impossibilities the picture of chaos her life had begun to embody. And in a deliberate confession of raw faith, she held out her palms, elbows extended, and slowly lifted that two-handed bowl of brokenness up to the Lord in surrender.

He was right. She couldn't do it. This mess was His to fix and figure out.

And He has.

He does.

Because this is how we were meant to live out the ramifications of good gone bad gone amazingly good again through the introduction of the gospel into our world and into our lives. We yield. We surrender. We don't try to force our fixes. We don't continue in worry and fear, nor in bitterness and bad attitudes, nor in self-willed attempts to gain God's favor in hopes of regaining the relief of His blessings. No, we valiantly raise up our dust-to-dust handfuls of broken pieces, assured by faith that the same gospel which drew us to Him for salvation is the same gospel that will keep saving us going forward—saving us from what our world and others and even ourselves have done to destroy what God has redeemed. We face today's challenges and our own sense of emptiness with the same "I can't do it" dependence on Christ that first embraced the eternal forgiveness of our sins.

Otherwise, we're just keeping ourselves in the same old fix.

Chapter 2

Attempted Redemption

A Morality Play in Four Acts

There are people, obviously, who don't want anything to do with God, Jesus, the Bible, religion, church, change, the whole smash. The gospel may mean "good news" by definition, in preacher's terms, but not by the way the dictionary reads at their house. They've got their own ways of dealing with life . . . and God's not one of them.

But despite every delusion to the contrary, the downdraft from the previous chapter you just read is that while the good news of the gospel may not *appeal* to everyone, the *bad* news of the gospel still *applies* to everyone. So even if a person might never be willing to admit it directly to anyone's face, none of us can escape the universal, underlying sense of displeasure and disappointment we all feel for life on the ground—not all day every day perhaps, but often and intensely enough at times that each of us flares up with the urge to do something about it, to cope with it, to make it go away.

To fix it.

We're fixers.

It's how we try changing the dynamic. It's how we try creating our own redemption.

Now listen, we're not judging here, because we've all done it, and we all still do it. For even though the gospel of Christ, received by faith, removes all need for us to keep our stash of fix-it stuff on hand, the fact remains that most of our attics and basements and garages still have a number of buckets we pull out when things aren't going the way we like. Some of them we only use as needed, from time to time. Others, however, have become a regular part of our day. Our M.O. Our maintenance plan.

But the only change or result that any of them produce—the only change they *can* produce—is change for the worst. What you'll see in the four buckets we're about to bring out into the open is that no matter how much we may feel dependent on them or drawn to them for the support they give us and for the quick fixes they some-times provide, they eventually bottom out, dry up, and quit working.

They're wasted runs at redemption.

God help us for thinking they'll ever be anything more.

I. Ourselves

Hard to believe it, based on our highly sketchy track record, but we have thoroughly convinced ourselves that the cure for what's wrong with us is the well-oiled creation of a better version of us. Somewhere in our heads is a future person with our same razor and toothbrush who, once he or she finally gets here—the embodiment of self-disciplined, self-defined perfection—that guy or that girl is going to turn our whole world right-side-up.

Okay, a little diagnostic question for you: Ten years ago, you thought that person would be here by today, didn't you? Didn't you? (Slight pause here for effect, waiting for your silent answer.) Yeah, that's what we thought. Well, wonder what happened to him? Wonder what happened to her? If that new image is not who you've been able to become by now, after all this time, what makes you really think you're going to become that person by tomorrow morning or by a week from next Sunday?

The truth is (and come on now, you know this) you would be hard-pressed to find *anyone—AN-Y-ONE—*over the course of your lifetime who has lied to you, and fought you, and failed you, and disgusted you more than *you* have. Right? And that's the person you're counting on to come to your rescue? That's the one who's going to figure it all out and turn things around for you? Serious? An improved version of you?

Boy, do we people ever not get it.

It doesn't matter who'll be drinking out of your coffee cup when you're twenty-five, or thirty-five, or sixty-five, or eighty-five, that person is going to be a rank disappointment to you. Doesn't matter how ripped his abs are, doesn't matter how much money she makes, doesn't matter how high he's climbed the ladder, or how nice she looks in a little black dress. That tight, together, attractive person—the one you keep envisioning in your head—still isn't going to do it for you. We promise you.

You don't think so?

Well, let's hear your logic then, your comeback, if you've got any evidence to the contrary. Ever been happy with this person so far? For any length of time? Ever known yourself to be completely satisfied with your weight, your build, your time management choices, or your success at self-denial? Your habits, your hairstyle, your dedication, your ability level? And has there ever been any reason why you couldn't make any of these things happen the way you wanted? If you really wanted to?

As if you really could? To your total satisfaction?

We are so good at fooling ourselves. We are so sure that we can become the person who makes ourselves happy, complete, content, and confident. But even while we're breathing the scented smoke of our own betterment plans—declaring this self-hyped person to be a better god than God is, applauding our independence and sovereignty—we are simultaneously proving to be our own worst enemy.

We're just crazy that way.

No, it's actually even worse than that. According to the Bible, "Cursed is the man who trusts in man and makes flesh his strength, whose heart turns away from the LORD." *Cursed.* "He is like a shrub in the desert, and shall not see any good come. He shall dwell in the parched places of the wilderness, in an uninhabited salt land" (Jer. 17:5–6).

Whew, that's some tough talking.

But true . . . because you know good and well, from tons of past history, this is exactly where our little self-help programs always take us. To the desert. To the wilderness. You've been there before, haven't you? Like we have. You've woken up there on way too many mornings. You've crashed there on way too many drives home. You've shaken the desert sand out of just about every pair of shoes and piece of clothing you own. And as long as you keep looking to yourself as your next best solution, you will never stop vacuuming up the mess you leave behind. You will never be good enough to suit *yourself*, much less be good enough for God.

Because we cannot redeem ourselves.

2. Others

Nor can we do it through other people.

Take Beth's story, for example.

She grew up in a Christian home. Saved at age nine. But in middle school, the fears, self-doubts, and anxieties of adolescence had begun to cloud her view of God's redeeming love and His approval of her as His child. By the time she was seventeen, she'd intentionally changed her image to attract the attention of other boys and to fill her hunger for acceptance.

But only a few days into her senior year, the main boy she'd been able to attract with her new clothes and look and demeanor had sexually assaulted her. And so instead of just dealing with her old, normal, youthful insecurities anymore, those difficult-enough things were now sharing space in her heart with some all-new disruptions: shame, anger, self-hatred, things like that.

For this reason, Beth may not have been as drawn to the delusion, the way some of us are, that she could make herself into the person who satisfied her own deepest needs. But what she couldn't do for herself, she intended to go find in others. And before she'd completed college, she'd found the guy she wanted to marry and had tied the knot. *That'll fix it. That'll fix me.*

It took ten years and an ultimate separation before Beth fully realized she'd never healed from her past, that she'd draped her desperate hopes for identity and redemption around the shoulders of her husband. Marriage had only served to reinforce the width, height, and density of her emotional walls. And this man she loved—and who truly loved her—had proved unable to tear them down. Know the feeling? From one, both, or either side?

We could tell this same story in a hundred different ways, merely switching out the names and details, plugging in various relationship examples (friends, family, spouses, children), spicing up the personal elements with unique kinds of backgrounds and histories. And yet almost every account would end up tumbling toward the exact same place: a person looking to somebody else to fill what's missing inside.

Every divorce—and we're using that word "every" with deliberate intention, gleaned from much observation and experience—every divorce, at the broken part of its foundation, stems from placing an expectation on another person that he or she can never humanly achieve. Obviously a lot more is involved in marital conflict as well, but even the sinful, presenting symptoms of adultery, pornography, homosexuality—they're simply the deviant responses of a man or woman who perceives their mate should be filling their every need, and who feels forced to go out and get it through back channels when those needs are not met to their satisfaction.

You see this also when spouses become abusive, domineering, overbearing, controlling. It shows they haven't gotten what they both want and demand from their wife or husband, and so they're seeking to correct what he or she is not doing (in their opinion) to round out what they're expected to be.

Marriages will always struggle and will often fail whenever we make the person who wears our wedding ring into a god who's supposed to make us complete. And this same logic applies to every relationship we enter . . . for these very simple reasons:

Men make terrible gods.

Women make terrible gods.

Children make unholy terrible gods.

Friends, coworkers, parents, boyfriends/girlfriends, fiancés, you name it—whenever you look to another person to fill the thirsty cracks and crevices that are gaping open in your heart, you are moving not in the direction of freedom and healing, not into the experience of being full and satisfied, not into the hot tub of joy and pleasure. Instead, you're sailing straight into the headwinds of conflict and chaos and into cranked-up levels of personal pain.

The expectation that others can somehow become for us the answer to all our problems is to put an impossible weight on them that they were never intended, created, or equipped to carry. It's going to make life miserable for everybody.

Stop it. Please.

Because we can't be redeemed by others.

3. The World

Sometimes, on some days, in certain kinds of moods and situations, a carton of Blue Bell ice cream can work real magic on your soul. Suddenly, for those ten, delectable, moose-track minutes, the world just doesn't seem like such a problematic place as before.

Same thing goes when we walk out of the house sporting a new jacket or outfit, maybe a new computer device under our arm, or on those rare but, oh, so sweet occasions, a new ride to peel out of our driveway in. There's a brief window of time—rarely more than a week, usually much, much less—when we let this stuff convince us how smart and well-off we are, how much more complete and put-together than we were before these things were part of our lives.

In reality, of course, we're still the same guy, the same girl, only with less money in the bank and more debt on the way. But until those bills start rolling in, you'd never know it from the look in our eyes and the swagger in our step. It's all good.

Feeling much better now.

Guess what, though. It's sort of the same cunning way some person's going to feel at around 9:30 one Saturday morning, several years from now, when they drive away from the curb at your house with that same watch and kitchen appliance and sport coat and desk lamp and whatever else at your garage sale they talked you down to fifty cents for. The things of this world—no matter what cool shape of toy or trinket they assume—are all on a collision course with the junkyard at some point in their life cycles. That house you want, that raise you want, that truck you want, that new living room suite you want. They will not hold up. They can't maintain the straight face of a mood change for very long.

But try telling that to most of us, and we'll take the fleeting feeling. We'll take it in exchange for reality on just about any day of the week—which means we'll be coming back to this faulty well again and again, needing our fix, seeking our sugar rush, only to be sadly disappointed for the millionth time by how quickly we're slurping the bottom of the milk shake glass . . . and back at the counter ordering more.

It's really no different from what Dr. William Silkworth observed in terms of alcohol addiction and abuse. Writing in what's now known as the "Big Book" of Alcoholics Anonymous, he talked about people feeling irritable and restless, disconnected, discontent, then they see others who appear to be finding a sense of relief and acceptance for themselves through guilt-free, uninhibited drinking. Soon they're trying it themselves—for the purpose of satisfying those empty cravings inside—only to be caught up in a miserable cycle of insanity, endlessly returning to what temporarily chills their lack of contentment.

Pick your poison. It's all the same desire.

The problem with these sorts of worldly pursuits—and we'll deal with this more fully in the next chapter—is not that the activity we're enjoying (whether food or sex or shopping or whatever) is infused with innate moral wrong. On the contrary, food and sex and material enjoyments are part of what God has created for our pleasure and use.

But when we go buy things with money we don't have because we're greedy for how they make us feel . . .

When we pull into the drive-thru because we're lonely and upset, and a double cheeseburger just really settles us down . . .

When we're dying for sex because we're low in the confidence and approval tank and jittery from our own insecurity . . .

We're using the gifts of God as if they themselves are gods. We're chasing them beyond the proper, beneficial boundaries where we were designed by God to enjoy them, deciding instead that these items and activities can satisfy us all by themselves. We're elevating created things above their Creator.

And even though they fail us every bit as readily as we fail ourselves, even though they prove just as incapable of fulfilling us as all the other people do in our lives, we still keep pushing that gimme button like blasted morons, fully expecting that the next time we snag whatever comes out of it will be the time when the satisfaction finally takes hold, when the good feelings finally stick around and stay. And so like clockwork, we go down in flames again and again to our alcohol abuse or our sexual lust or our sweet tooth or our credit line—whatever particular desire is so powerful and predictable at deceiving us. We grab for things that have never failed to disappoint us in the past, thinking that what we must need more than anything is *more* of it . . . more of the same thing that's never been able to satisfy us before.

That's the call of the world for you. And it's madness.

Because the world doesn't have what it takes to redeem us.

4. Religion

Just wanted you to know—especially if you're still somewhat cynical toward the gospel—we're not putting ourselves and some of our churchy ways above all scrutiny either. Religious attempts at redemption are no more failed and foolish than the ones where you try to solve your problems by getting better at being *you*.

In fact, when we try to tilt the scales of God's favor to our advantage by checking off the standard good-Christian boxes, aren't we just running a 2.0 version of #1—"redeeming ourselves"—the only difference being that we're dressing it up in Sunday clothes and a choir robe, working it out to the tune of a praise band?

By the way, let's set the record straight on this "scales" business once and for all. Can't tell if this comes as good news or a surprise to you or not, but these scales we keep trying to tip in our direction? The scales that God uses to measure how we're doing? The scales that tell whether He's happy with us or not?

Those scales don't exist. There *are* no scales. You're either completely justified by the blood of Jesus Christ, or you're not justified at all. It's that simple.

There are hundreds if not thousands of reasons why living the way God's Word teaches and describes for us is the smart, wholesome, healthy way to go about it. Fearing and worshiping Him with our grateful obedience is a beautiful thing that comes with all kinds of fatherly blessings attached. But doing it to attract God's attention or to get on His good side is not even *one* of those reasons, nor is it the toggle switch for even *one* of those blessings. Striving for His honor roll by handing in a good report card is as ludicrous as trying to force our way to fulfillment by demanding it from others or expecting it from the world.

Religion doesn't work.

Just like none of the other three works.

Trying to earn God's pleasure *does not work.*

And yet it goes on all the time. All over the place. Look at any of the major monotheistic religions of the world. Tell us what you see. You see a system of thought where people perform certain acts or rites or scheduled ceremonies, hoping to keep their accounts paid up so they can one day turn them in for final redemption. Cashing in their chips. And it is so silly, these lists of things—especially when they become the way that saved-by-grace *Christians* try relating to God.

This tilting-the-scales stuff is based on the very unbiblical idea that good little boys and girls are the ones who go to heaven. In reality, it's *bad* little boys and girls transformed by the gospel of Jesus Christ who go to heaven—those whose sins are covered by His redeeming work, and who love Him so much because of it, they live now to flesh out these new desires He's placed within them as a way of expressing their willing worship.

Not to buy their way inside, but to celebrate *being* inside.

Because we can never be redeemed by religion.

Roots and Fruit

When you pick up a book like this one that talks about "how to change"—says it right there on the cover—the *one thing* in your life that you've decided needs changing the most is almost certainly the *one thing* that's most on your mind.

Maybe for you, that "one thing" is a nasty addiction you've been battling for years and years, for as long as you can remember. Maybe it's a depression that just keeps rolling over you in waves, hardly ever letting up, beating you down until you've started to doubt the love of God, the love of anybody. Maybe it's a damaged relationship, maybe past episodes of abuse that have tainted the way you think, act, and respond, so much that you don't always even recognize yourself or the person you've become as a result.

Whatever it is, you *know* what it is.

"I have a drug problem," you may say.

"I have an overeating problem."

"I have a lust problem."

"My relationships don't work."

And since you say so, it's probably true. But what you *really* have—what all of us have, by birth—is more than anything a heart problem. And if you're trying to treat the "one thing" in your life by (1) trying harder, (2) using others, (3) escaping, or (4) upping your religion quotient—or any combination of these—all you're really doing is just mowing over the weeds. You're trimming things up, making them look almost okay for a little while. But just wait—they'll be coming back in full force before you know it, in all their scraggly, tangled variety. They may be laying low for a little while, but don't kid yourself. They still have the run of your yard and your property. And they still have all kinds of openings and options for creeping back up on you . . . some that you don't even know about yet.

These weeds are the kinds of wild grass that naturally grow from your inheritance of Adam's bloodline, as well as from your willing alliance with him in rebellion against God. What you're seeing above the ground is simply evidence of the damning and the damage that have occurred—with your full, outright permission—down in the biochemistry of your life.

It goes back to what Jesus said: "There is nothing outside a person that by going into him can defile him"—in other words, we're not made *unclean* by the things we do, allow, or entertain, but rather, He said, "the things that come out of a person are what defile him" (Mark 7:15). We haven't made ourselves sinners; sin is what's already inside us. As we like to say it, "the heart of our problem is the problem of our hearts."

And for this job, we need a root canal. We need to let God get down underneath what we *think* needs changing, so that He can bring full restoration and redemption to us where we *truly* need changing.

Example: We've learned over the years that for men who struggle with laziness or who lack initiative—when that's what their weed profile and presentation looks like—the root cause behind what they're living out is actually fear. They're not as inactive so much as they're afraid—afraid of failing, afraid of risking, afraid they're not good enough, afraid they would only succeed at falling short if they tried any harder than they're doing. Make sense?

We've observed, too, that people (both men *and* women) who give in to pornography addictions are motivated by the twin urges of anger and control, springing up from the idolatrous roots of lustful fantasy. They're insecure, angered over certain life experiences, fueled by a desire to turn the tables and exercise control over their lives and over others' lives. As a result, they begin to dehumanize the visible images of men and women made in the image of God, using them for their own pleasure under the power of their own will.

Many other types of weeds grow up the same way. They're always less characterized by the colors and shapes of what we see above ground, and more by (let's say) an underlying lack of forgiveness, for instance, that has twisted its way up through the grass line in the shape of blame or abuse, relational difficulty, loneliness. See what we mean? We could go on and on like this, diagnosing the presence of sinful or destructive fruit by the actual root system that keeps it fed and fueled underground.

We're just saying that our core issues—and again, we're talking about all of us, not just you or a certain subset of people—the big issues of life that need changing are much more serious than we tend to think . . . more serious than even the joy-robbing habits, addictions, and experiences we recognize on the surface and wish to run from.

It's terminal. We're toast.

Beyond any manufactured forms of redemption.

And if you might just stop trying to defend your allegiances to the hurt you've endured, to the anger you deserve, to the blame you've placed, to the revenge you're carrying, to the fear you rationalize, to the battle positions you refuse to give up . . .

And if you'll begin to recognize that you, like everyone, are diseased at the roots, incapable of effecting your own release and rescue, aware that all your attempts at redemption amount to pouring your best hopes into "broken cisterns that can hold no water" (Jer. 2:13) . . .

Then please hear us say: This admission of need and reality is a good thing. This is where the stuff you hate the most about yourself can go to die. This is how the High Surgeon of heaven begins performing the corrective procedures on your heart that can ultimately set you free.

This is how you change.

Chapter 3

Full Recovery

The Gospel of Jesus Christ

Randy and his wife, Cindy, were already reeling from the steady pummeling of several life-altering setbacks: job loss, health problems, a miscarriage, all within a short space of time. Then came the dark, cold night of December 26, late that same year—the night that snuffed out what little was left of their thirteen-year marriage—when Randy, unable to shake the guilt of a long-ago affair, chose the quiet of this Christmas moment to admit what he had done.

You can only imagine.

Or perhaps you can imagine all too well.

Cindy—understandably destroyed—packed up her things and went to stay with her sister, while Randy was left alone to stare face to face at the four-wall reality he'd been unwilling to see in himself before. Compromises in character, accountability, and integrity had been agonizingly exposed (as they always will), and now he was living with the dreadfully lonely and shameful consequences. Though his feet had been dragging bottom for a long time, the numbing effects of denial and blame had been able to dull the sensation of raw, scraping flesh. But now, in the starkness of an empty house, he was feeling the pain, seeing the carnage.

"While we were still weak," the Bible says, "at the right time . . ."

Another example is Beau, one of the elders in our church, who became a Christian as a college freshman, and immediately began serving Him, loving Him, being changed by Him. One of the markers in his spiritual growth was a rich, biblical understanding of what's wrong with the human heart—the kinds of things we've been talking about so far in this book—how we're broken in the deepest places, and how we instinctively look everywhere else but to God to calm our agitation and restlessness.

Beau actually had been diagnosed with clinical depression as early as eight years old, and had struggled with its leaden weight into adulthood, into marriage, even into his years of walking faithfully with the Lord. And yet he'd begun to wonder—not that he felt condemned for remaining on prescription meds to control his brain chemistry, but—"What if there's something in my heart that needs to be addressed," he thought, "something that these antidepressants are masking? What would it hurt me, just for a season, just to see?"

Answer: It would hurt *bad*. Immediately upon weaning himself off his pills, the depression cratered to all-new levels of darkness. Unbelievable despair. Brutal. Although surrounded by his wife, his church, and capable counseling, the undertow of his thoughts and emotions effectively buried him in the subflooring. With hardly a breath of relief or reprieve.

The sun barely shone for two full years in his life. He can't even exactly remember where he was, or what he was doing, the day something approaching brightness and warmth actually caught his surprised attention. But he does remember when he cognitively recognized that he was trusting the Lord, like never before, that he was being drawn toward hope by the purest sense of God's love and favor he'd ever known, that he'd not only been redeemed through the one-time work of Christ, but was even then—and is still, even now—continually experiencing redemption.

For "while we were still weak," and at just "the right time . . ."

Then there's Ashley, a preacher's kid, but who always had a big hole in her heart for love and attention. It had gotten her into lots of trouble along the way, and into a number of abusive relationships, taking her far away from the person she'd seen herself being and becoming.

But something happened one day at the funeral of her youth pastor, who'd been tragically killed in a car accident. It was so sad. The whole thing had been shocking. But everything people said about him—and all of it was so true—was how much he loved Jesus, how passionately he followed Jesus, how infectiously he lived for Jesus. And all Ashley could think was, if she'd been the one who'd died early instead of him, nobody would be saying those same things about her. She wouldn't have been surprised, honestly, if almost nobody even showed up. There wasn't really much to celebrate or remember or admire.

Especially after the wedding incident. She'd been asked to be the maid of honor for a friend, and had been excited to be included as such a key part of the big day. But in the weeks leading up to the ceremony, Ashley had started drinking heavily. She'd gotten to be embarrassing and disruptive. And in a couple of fits of anger and attitude, she had done a good job of wrecking the friendship between herself and the soon-to-be bride.

Other friends were telling the other girl that she'd be within her rights never to speak to Ashley again, much less feel bad about cutting her out of the wedding party, even at this late date. But instead, she approached Ashley with forgiveness and grace. She spent time, even with the busy season of preparations in full swing, talking things over with her and seeing how she could help. Most of all, she told her that her love for her, just like Jesus' love for both of them, was greater than any sin, any fault, or any attempts to push the other away.

Because "while we were still weak"—when the time was just right—"Christ died for the ungodly."

Gotta love you some Romans 5:6. You've gotta love what you hear the God of glory and all creation say to you and to us about what He was willing to do to redeem us from enemy status— "while we were still sinners" (v. 8)—and what He keeps on doing every day to redeem those who "have now been justified by his blood" (v. 9) so that we can continue, even as believers, to be "saved by his life" (v. 10).

Love it.

Yes, love it.

Are we really that weak? You'd better believe we're that weak. People talk about Christianity being a crutch, like they're really laying the wood to our backsides, like that's really supposed to hurt us.

But that statement has never bothered us. We're like, "Absolutely." We _need_ that crutch. Couldn't _make_ it without that crutch. Because get this: leaning on the crutch of Christianity sure beats hobbling around without help on a busted femur, which is the only choice we were ever going to get unless God had come charging in here at the right time, while we were weak, and propped us up by the living power of Jesus' death and resurrection.

People ask, "So are you saying we're all just damned? There's nothing we can do? That's it? From the moment we're born?" Yeah, that's pretty much what we're saying.

"We can't change, then? We're not capable of living right? We can't see what's wrong for ourselves and do what it takes to correct it?" Nope. That's kind of the deal.

Unless . . .

. . . unless God steps out onto the shattered glass of Randy and Cindy's marriage, and shows them what the gospel provides and what it can do, even twenty some-odd years later in a fully redeemed relationship with each other.

. . . unless God goes down with Beau into the hellish depths of depression, not shaming a church leader for not being able to shake off the bad moods any better than this, but rather carrying him through with tender toughness.

. . . unless God uses the unconditional love of a friend to reflect the character of Christ in Ashley's life, transforming a young woman who saw herself as dirty, despised, and disrespected into a welcomed, unashamed daughter of the King.

The beauty of Christ's gospel is the great "unless" of life.

Here's how we've seen it play out in *our* lives . . .

Matt

I've shared some of my story in print before, but quickly again here: I reached high school before I was truly confronted in any kind of healthy gospel fashion with who Jesus is. My mom was faithful to the Lord, despite some legalistic hang-ups she brought with her into adulthood, so I knew some things about Christ from an early age. Knew what I liked and *didn't* like.

But God used a few faithful men to show me His love and truth up close through their interest in me and their example while I was growing up. Then a football teammate of mine, who wouldn't back away from sharing Jesus with me—right there in the locker room—turned out to be very key in God's "right time" providence in my life, cracking open the skeptical, doubtful resistance of my young heart.

I didn't really have any business playing football. I was lanky and awkward and uncoordinated. (Not much has changed.) I did most of my playing by pretending to be the *other* team in practice, rather than playing on *our* team in the actual games. Jeff, however, was a star—went on to play college ball, in fact. The real deal. But even though I wasn't exactly in his league athletically, he invited me to church with him: "Would you like to come this Wednesday night?"

"No, I really don't think I would," was my first response.

But I finally did. And while what I saw through one eye was a bunch of lame geeks and weirdos, singing corny songs and spelling out words with their bodies, what I saw through the other eye were imperfect people, every bit as train wrecked as I was, yet pursuing God full-on with their hearts and lives and being changed by what He was doing inside them.

And yet, despite whatever attraction I may have been feeling toward Christ and His gospel during those days, weeks, and months, my protective fallback remained the same: looking sideways at anything that screamed biblical or religious. I was a lot more interested in disproving Christianity than being intrigued by it. I was always trying to locate the loopholes and exemptions that kept me from having to seriously think about submitting to it. But even with my state of mind still pushing back and not wanting to go there, it was almost as if Jesus just finally got tired of playing nice with me, and said, "Get in here, boy. You know you're Mine."

He'd won. I gave in.

And when I did, I gave in hard.

He just completely evaporated my heat shield, and completely captivated my affections for Him and His Word. He saw through the weakness of my arguments and all my defenses, and "right timed" me right into His kingdom with a new heart that He made hungry to follow Him and be changed by His all-consuming grace.

Michael

My story, I'll warn you, is quite a bit different.

I relapsed in drug treatment on New Year's Eve, the night before the new millennium—the ultimate moment of a lifetime, you'd think, for turning over a new leaf. And while it would prove to be my last using experience, it felt at the time as if I was never getting out of that trap. I couldn't see much hope on the horizon for somebody in my shape.

I'd been married. Had a little girl. Made a lot of money in commercial real estate. But drugs and alcohol had slowly but surely destroyed everything meaningful in my life, including what I'd known and understood about God, having been raised in and around the church as a kid. At thirty-two, I was divorced, depressed, despondent, and—after a reckless traffic accident that left me hospitalized—I was completely alone. Some of the members of my family didn't give me six more months to live, the way I was going. And who could blame them? I'd given them no reason to think otherwise.

But there, in probably the weakest moment of what had been many, many years of weak moments, God began to step in. The counselor who'd been assigned to my case, speaking with me a few days later—early January 2000—told me he believed I'd been given a calling by God, a mission that required a different kind of life than the one I'd been leading. Honestly, there wasn't any Jesus in what he was saying, just as there hadn't been any Jesus in anything I'd heard throughout my whole time in that facility. But He was there, where He routinely is found—around the fringes of society.

And when I returned to my room, closed the door, God shined a light into my dark heart. Completely exposed what was hidden underneath. I had never felt so much sorrow and grief. Nor had I ever felt so much hope and love. Honestly, I didn't understand what was happening to me. I even went around the building in the days following, talking about being part of a "revolution"—which tends to make the security staff at a rehab center a little nervous! But that's how drastically Christ had begun what would later become clear to me was a radical, saving encounter with the living God.

It didn't end all my problems. There was still wreckage strewn around in my life and in many people's lives. But God had now entered into it. He had loved me in my weakness.

Strength in Weakness

When compared with each other perhaps, we may only seem weak by degrees—enough that we might even consider ourselves relatively strong and self-supporting. But when placed before Almighty God and before our heavy, inborn curse of sinfulness, we are weak by utter default. All of us.

So if you struggle with being able to run hard after the Lord because you feel *so* unworthy, *so* unclean, *so* unsteady, listen up: "While [you] were still weak, at the right time," God came to your rescue. And still does. And still is.

If you just cannot accept, no matter how many times we say it, that God takes sheer delight in you, even though you're stumbling around in your failures and addictions and making such slow strides toward maturity—hear us: "God shows his own love for us in that, while we were still sinners, Christ died for us."

No way, of course, does He want you to keep being beaten up and taken hostage by these unsightly habits and other leftover dysfunctions. They mean you no good, and they will always cost you freedom and joy and the confident blessings of obedience. But that doesn't mean we're not all, every last one of us, in an ongoing recovery mode as God keeps doing His work in us—which, dang, we must sure need a lot of.

Perhaps you were saved early in life. Perhaps the Lord Jesus found you while you were just calmly sitting in Sunday school class, not strung out on a bender or at the badly frayed end of your rope. Man, that's the testimony we want for all of our children— that they would never know anything other than loving Him and pursuing Him, rejoicing in what He has done in Christ to make them part of His covenant family. Praise the Lord for sparing you some of the God-awful sights and sounds experienced by some of His kids, the dank and unspeakable places He has required His love to go in order to snag some of us out of our hellholes.

But here's guessing, no matter where He found you, you've felt some serious weakness along the way. Maybe, in fact, you've never felt quite as weak as you feel right this minute. Then be thankful your redemption isn't a one-off—a one-time moment in your teens or childhood that you're afraid might not have been front-loaded with enough grace to accommodate what you've done with it in the meantime.

That's exactly what the Bible does *not* say. God still has a plan for you, weak though you may be . . . weak though we all are. His love and acceptance of you, His pride at giving you His name, and His joyful interest in what He's continuing to fashion in you as He leads you along in life—these promises and many more are yours by His own heavenly choice. And nothing but the old, shopworn lies of the Enemy are what's keeping you from falling back full-weight—ropes course-style—into your loving Savior's embrace, experiencing in flesh and blood and Friday night victory what He's fought and died and lives again to give you.

So, no, you're right—not all the dark spaces went away when you succumbed to the call of His grace and received Him by faith.

But the good news of His eternal gospel is still working reconnaissance and going in for the invasion . . . and is looking mighty strong, if we say so ourselves, especially against your (and our) weakness.

Retrofitting

For some reason, which we ought to find very hard to understand, we can read and hear stories like these of rescue and perseverance, we can read and hear the gospel truth proclaimed through God's Word and from the pulpit, and . . . well . . . we still kind of feel like our "attempted redemptions" stand a little better chance of working out for us.

It's insane. It is.

But it's us. Isn't it?

And yet if we're really listening to the gospel—which tells us that "for our sake he made him to be sin who knew no sin, so that in him we might become the righteousness of God" (2 Cor. 5:21)—we ought to begin to see a difference in how we cash that out. If we can begin to slow down our excuses and our reflexes long enough to acclimate toward what's truly being said in the Scriptures, we may actually start to forget where we used to keep those fixer-upper buckets and solutions of ours. We can straighten out these crooked wells where we've been trying to draw up our own sense of security and pain relief. We won't do it perfectly, of course, but we can at least do it much less stupidly.

And then, we might just start seeing some changes.

Let's take another swing through those four things again, making note of what the gospel's done to them.

Ourselves

No longer, for instance, should we *ever* be conned into thinking we can do good all by ourselves . . . because even on our *best* days, we fall woefully short of God's expectations of us.

Ask yourself what you ever did to pull yourself out of the muck and mire of your sin. Wasn't it God (not you) yanking hard on the business end of that rope, the one that sprung you free from the mess you'd made . . . and from all the messes you've kept on making?

Have you ever read Psalm 18? Psalm 40? (You do know the gospel is all over the Old Testament, right?) Check out what happens when God responds to His people's desperation, how He comes barreling out of heaven, thundering through the clouds, picking up so much speed that His incoming approach peels back sprayed layers of sea water, exposing a dry channel through the ocean bed—all to rescue us from an enemy that is "too mighty" for us, to snatch us out of death's swamp-like grip and set our feet safely "on a rock."

Go read it. Blows your mind.

So where's the rationale for Christian pride and presumption, seeing as that's all the hand you ever played in your salvation? Where does all this woof-woofing come from, like you're scaring off the bad guys, swaggering out into the octagon cage?

Get *over* yourself. You were saved by grace alone through faith alone. Therefore, God gets all the glory alone. And when you understand this one basic issue, you'll stop going into *you* and start going into the Lord—just laying out all the smelly, rotten groceries, shaking all the stuff out of your pockets, bringing it all out into the open, and saying, "Here, would You please get rid of this for me?" If your spouse or your kids or your boss or your parents ever pick out a piece of your character or attitude that needs fixing, you just take your pitiful self straight before Him and say, "Jesus, come and get it."

Because your satisfaction comes from *His* work, not yours.

Others

A lot of us swing up or down almost solely on the basis of others' acceptance and validation of us. When we get it from them, we're good. But if not, then we're nervous, we're self-conscious. Sometimes we're hot about it, or else moody and unhappy, almost unable to function.

But not when the gospel's securely in place in our heads. Your and our approval comes from God, not from them—not from your friends, your coworkers, your competitors, your critics—because at best, their opinions have a very limited shelf life. Those people are one step closer to death today just like you are. The only one whose approval should matter to you is the One you'll stand before in judgment someday. And He's already declared you redeemed.

Sounds like, then, His opinion is all you need, which means you just need to be a lot more tuned into that than into what anybody else is saying.

God's rescue of us, coupled with His acceptance of us, enables us to walk in one fluid motion of humility and confidence. These two qualities, within the context of gospel living, can begin to glide right along with each other, until they almost become one and the same thing. In humility, we don't go around doing whatever we want, whenever we want, unwilling to respond repentantly or circumspectly to any kind of rebuke. And yet in confidence, we're not dictated by the poll results of those around us. We're not saying things and doing things merely to keep our approval numbers up. Our approval grades are already settled. The books are already closed. Now we can just live to serve and worship and lead and love and relax and enjoy the blessings of God.

So instead of needing your wife or husband to think you're awesome before you feel motivated to love and care for them—no, their favorable opinion of you is not your highest good. You are as loved by God on the days when your spouse thinks you hung the moon as on those days when you think they'd really just like to hang you. The way they respond to you doesn't determine the way you treat them, the way you remain obedient to the Lord, or the decisions you make on behalf of your family.

Because your satisfaction comes from *Him*, not from them.

The World

Our problem with the world is not the world. One of the main reasons why we pinball from one bad habit to another, caught in this endless ricochet of highs and lows—feeling good about ourselves, feeling horrible about ourselves, feeling in control one minute, feeling enslaved the next—is because we keep looking to worldly things to fill us up. And that's not what they're there for.

More importantly, as redeemed people, that's not what we *need* them for.

Look at it this way: Just because something exists in "the world"—outside of worship service and Bible study—doesn't put it on the Christian's no-no list. God, in what's known as His *common grace* toward all people (differentiated from His *saving grace,* which forgives our sin and effectuates the gospel) provides us with all kinds of things that anyone can enjoy, Christian or otherwise.

Food, for example, tastes as good to a pagan as it does to a Presbyterian. There's nothing inherently evil about a fillet, or a chili dog, or potato chips, or Double Stuf Oreos. Questionable nutritional values maybe, in some of those, but not confessional sin material necessarily. Food is something provided by God to *all* of us for our nourishment and delight.

Same thing goes for sex, which is obviously another gift from God that doesn't require the prerequisite of church membership before it's able to be enjoyed, before a person is likely to take interest in it. I think we can deduce from Jennifer Love Hewitt movies and Super Bowl commercials that all kinds of people are into this kind of thing.

Same goes for wine, which (we know this can get a little controversial, in some circles, but—) it's part of God's good creation that Scripture doesn't warn us away from, except as it leads to drunkenness. And obviously, again, the world has a connoisseur taste for this as well.

But here's the gospel difference . . .

An unsaved person (as well as the Christian who goes around thinking like one) eats a big meal, enjoys a nice glass, makes love to his wife, and . . . here's where it breaks down: that worldly moment of gratification is as good as it's ever going to get. They'll wake up Saturday morning, no matter how expensive the dinner was, no matter how lovely their time in the bedroom was, and they'll still be needing more. They'll still be unsatisfied.

But not us. Not if we're thinking right. By means of the gospel, through which God has chosen to delight in us and has given us all things to enjoy—within, of course, the healthy, discerning boundaries of wisdom and common sense—every gift of common grace represents a fresh, new opportunity for us to celebrate His wonder, His mercy, and His glory. *He* is the one—not our ample income or our remarkably good looks—who is responsible for these blessings. *He* is the one who created into His world such a wide color palette of flavors and textures, of aromas and pleasures. And so *He* is the one to be worshiped and thanked and glorified every time we experience even the most basic of His material gifts.

When properly viewed within this gospel frame, neither our desire for these things nor our expected payoff of what they can do for us terminates on the gift itself, but rather rolls up from there into praise and gratitude for who God is and what He's done.

And we leave feeling *totally* satisfied. In Him.

Religion

Among the things to finally be killed off in us, thanks to the invasive influence of the gospel in our lives, this religion-for religion's-sake nonsense is maybe the sweetest pass-through of all.

Let's field dress this thing and turn it into supper.

We're not letting it chase us or scare us anymore.

Religion is always outside-in. "I'll do something for You, God, and You do something for me." But come on now. Do you not see how backwards and idiotic that is? The gospel goes from the inside out. It is "Christ in you, the hope of glory" (Col. 1:27). A new heart, a new creation, new desires, new loves. Holiness and righteousness has been imputed to you—reborn inside of you—and nothing you can do can earn you any more favor than that.

See what this perspective does to your praying, your worship, your quiet time with the Lord? Sure, these things still require a battle of self-discipline oftentimes, since we remain in the process of learning how to quiet those lazy, deceptive voices inside ourselves. But we're not seeking God to get a sticker from Him or an attaboy. We're seeking Him to enjoy even greater intimacy with Him, to get even closer to His heart, to open more and more of those inner closets where we've tried to restrict access to Him, thinking He wouldn't like what He sees, thinking He might reject us if He knew.

The reason why we study His Word, why we attack our sin, why we share generously from our resources, and why we serve the people around us is not to *persuade* Him to love us. We do these things because He already *does* love us . . . and because He wants us to dig even deeper into the treasury of His blessing, into the joy and sweetness and abundant living His gospel unlocks for us.

There's your satisfaction for you.

From Death to Life

Remember that passage we mentioned a while ago from Jeremiah 17—the one about trusting in ourselves, about the desert and the wilderness? As is so often true in Scripture, the bad is contrasted against the good, the warning alongside the promise.

And here's the encouraging back half of those verses. "Cursed is the man," you'll recall, "who trusts in man and makes flesh his strength." That's the first part. But "blessed is the man who trusts in the LORD," who puts all his confidence in what God has done and can do, in all the places where we haven't and can't. That man or woman, the Bible says . . .

> . . . is like a tree planted by water, that sends out its roots by the stream, and does not fear when heat comes, for its leaves remain green and is not anxious in the year of drought, for it does not cease to bear fruit. (Jer. 17:8)

One of those types of trees, which factors into the biblical narrative all the way from Noah's ark to the Revelation, is the olive tree, which is notable for several interesting reasons. One is just how incredibly gnarly and twisted it can grow, especially the ones that are hundreds of years old, sometimes more than a thousand years old. Thick, squatty, weather-beaten trunks—as if they really have an interesting story to tell. Check out a picture sometime, you'll see what we're talking about.

But perhaps the most remarkable thing about an olive tree is that, even if the above-ground structure completely dies—dead limbs, no growth, brown, curled-up leaves, time to fire up the stump grinder—its root system is so hardy and strong, a living tree can actually resurrect from one that was totally destroyed and decayed.

The olive tree is a living picture of the gospel. It's redemption in action. Life doesn't reignite itself out on the branches, with tape and string and splices from other saplings. Instead it happens underground, out of sight, out of anyone's control, down where (unlike the olive tree) even our *roots* are dead. But God brings the rebirth. He restores what can't be restored. He takes what is brittle and broken and beyond all hope, and infuses His own life into dead spaces.

Not just once, but again and again. Ever renewing. Ever revitalizing.

Ever redeeming.

Ever satisfying.

That's the gospel.

Chapter 4

Struggling Well

True Faith in Real Life

Anybody who's ever played in a band or orchestra probably knows the unsettling feeling of being out of step with the music. Whether from taking your eyes off the conductor, miscounting the notes and rests, or simply not knowing which measure is coming next, the group can be plowing ahead around you, and you're too much out of sync to know when to come in.

If you lag too far behind, you'll likely be the only one at the downbeat who's not playing. But if you guess too soon, you could be the only one who *is* playing—*[squeak!]*—way out in front of everybody else. And you know it wasn't supposed to be a solo there.

That's what comes from being off-track.

And whether you mean to or not, you can get off-track with the gospel song too. Instead of letting it lead you to the place where its Writer originally intended—toward grateful worship of

God—you can follow it right out of its tempo markings and into confusion.

Like, for example, some people we know here in Texas think they're Christians because, well . . . they're from Texas. Or because they grew up going to church. Or because they were baptized when they were ten. And they've been doing their best ever since, living a pretty good life, trying to be a good person.

Well, good.

Good for them.

But being good doesn't make you a Christian, any more than being born in a conservative Southern state does, or having a granddaddy who's a preacher does, or being proud to be an American does. Becoming a Christian has nothing to do with being good or being brought up around reasonably good people. The gospel truth is that "no one does good, not even one" (Rom. 3:12). So all this "I'm good, I'm from Texas" good is just a bunch of nonsense—because, like we've said: *We're not the answer; we're the problem.*

That's off-track.

But what's equally out of whack is another specific line of thinking that is every bit as much a contradiction of who God is and what His gospel entails.

Can you be good enough to earn God's favor? Of course not.

But bad enough to lose it?

Can being bad make a Christian *not* a Christian?

Now before you go off thinking we're trying to sell the idea that it doesn't really matter how Christians live, let's get this straight. There's a reason why Jesus could say, using the agricultural terminology of His times, that the pathway to finding "rest for your souls" comes, not from roaming around doing whatever you want, but from hitching yourself up to His "yoke" and taking off from there. "For my yoke," He said, "is easy, and my burden is light" (Matt. 11:29–30).

Trust us on this one. Or remind yourself of it from your own ample experience. The "yoke" and "burden" of sin may not seem readily apparent or visible at first. But given enough time for the ugly buildup of regret and consequences to form, sin's yoke and burden is the absolute opposite of "easy" and "light." Whatever felt like freedom, pleasure, or innocent fun at the time ultimately turns into the furthest thing away from it.

I wish you could be a fly on the wall in some of the home groups or recovery groups at our church. The stories and memories and anguish you'd be hearing are often not even easy to *listen* to, much less knowing what it actually feels like to live it and be suffering the fallout. Maybe you're one of those stories yourself. Sin has done none of us any good, agreed? And it is sheer lunacy to think that the way to beat the spiritual system is to look pitiful enough one weekend to convince God to save you, then set out for the rest of your life to do whatever you feel like doing.

Even if that were an available option, that is *not* a good plan.

If you're a Christian who thinks you're missing out or have missed out on something by not experimenting with drugs or sleeping around, take it from people who know: heroin addictions and STDs are not the grand prizes of life, nor does their testimony drama outdo the sweet goodness of God that comes shining through your G-rated, nice-girl, nice-guy salvation story.

Are we clear on this? Sin is bad.

Always. For everybody.

Before salvation, *after* salvation.

It was the sin in our hearts, after all—inherited from Adam and then embraced as our own—that got us singing off-key in the first place, whistling straight down the tubes toward death and destruction. Until Jesus intervened. And by the gift of His righteousness, received when we believed on His name, He supernaturally put a new song in our hearts, cut us a new track, leading to life and joy and all the blessings of following Him.

Faith is what led us to repentance.

Jesus is who brought about change.

But this song doesn't play just long enough until you've found your seat in some heavenly game of musical chairs. And a lot of us fail to understand that, or at least to live and relate to God in conjunction with that. We start thinking our sin is bigger than God's redemptive power. We fear that by continuing to struggle with sin, it could mean the end of the line for us. But the proof of Christianity is not perfection. In fact, one of the key ways you can tell you're saved—as backwards as this logic may feel or sound—is when your faith is *continually* leading you toward repentance, and Jesus is *continually* bringing about change.

The ongoing response of a Christian to the gospel is a steady stream of ongoing repentance.

Repent!

People get the idea that *repentance* is primarily just hell-fire, street-preacher language, like a "TURN OR BURN" sign, stuck up on a tree trunk somewhere. "Repent!"—it's what all those weird-looking Old Testament prophets used to say, wearing their scratchy burlap, spitting out the words through yellowed teeth, shaking their bony fist in the air. "Repent!" (You nasty sinners.)

John the Baptist was like that, you may recall—an early New Testament throwback to the Elijahs of old. Camel skins for clothes. Matted hair for days. Crunchy locusts for breakfast. That's why we're not surprised to hear him saying to people on several occasions in Scripture to "repent," often just before calling them ugly names and making violent references to things like axes and vipers and fire and pitchforks.

But then finally—finally!—Jesus shows up on the scene. At long last we can be done with all the screaming and hollering. We fully expect the gentle Jesus to stride out onto the stage of human history, big smile on His face, and declare with a sweeping arm motion of magical love, "Don't worry, guys, you're all okay with Me."

And yet that's not what happened at all.

When He declared that His arrival on earth represented a significant fulfillment of Old Testament prophecy—when He declared at that moment "the kingdom of God is at hand"—He concluded this grand pronouncement by saying in no uncertain or inconsistent terms the same, one-word imperative that the long parade of prophets beforehand had given . . . with one important distinction. A strong, significant line that He added at the end. The one simple statement that makes repentance even possible.

"Repent," He said, "and believe in the gospel" (Mark 1:15).

The gospel, remember, means "good news." And for news to be good, as we said earlier, it must invade dark spaces, such as the dark, crooked paths we've already talked about: a futile trust in *ourselves*, a needy codependence on the approval of *others*, a tawdry love affair with the *world*, a pretend game of righteousness based on the rigid, arbitrary rules of *religion*.

Into each of these same dark spaces, Jesus was saying to the people of His day, just as He's said and is saying to us . . . *Repent and believe.*

But this repenting and believing is not merely a one-time occurrence. Sure, the gospel does involve an initial repentance from sin and belief in Jesus Christ. That's true. That's what we call salvation, regeneration, various other words in the biblical vocabulary. But "repent and believe" is much, much more than that. It is a foundational theme that continues forward in the life of a Christian. By means of the active, eternal grace of God, "repent and believe" becomes the living, growing, ever-renewing lifestyle of the Spirit-led believer.

Repent and believe.

Rinse and repeat.

This is a huge part of *Recovering Redemption*. It's how we ream out one of the main blockages in our spiritual arteries that keeps us from experiencing freedom in our life with Christ. Because despite what some people hypocritically think, being a follower of Jesus doesn't mean we never sin. (1 John 1:8: "If we say we have no sin, we deceive ourselves, and the truth is not in us.") But it does mean He has given us, by saving us, a heart that desires to turn back to Him . . . *when* we sin.

That's a big deal. And a big difference.

Anybody (obviously) can call themselves a Christian. They can want to be good, can wish they were different, can make any number of outside-in adjustments, trying to better themselves. But only a Christian has been given what he or she needs to truly hate their sin from the ground floor up, to desire true righteousness from the inside out, and to challenge what's truly wrong with themselves from a point of diagnostic clarity. To truly change. And the fruit of *repentance* is how we know it. In the same way we confirm the identity of an apple tree by noticing that apples are dangling from its branches, repentance growing up out of our hearts is a leading indicator of genuine belief on the inside. It shows us we're His from the roots up. Otherwise, we'd never go that deep.

"By this we know," the Bible says, "that we abide in him and he in us, because he has given us of his Spirit" (1 John 4:13)—the same Spirit who "searches everything, even the depths of God," who "comprehends the thoughts of God," who helps us "understand the things freely given us by God" (1 Cor. 2:10–12). And this Holy Spirit within us, who is constantly pumping us full of gospel truth and revelation—through His Word, through faithful preaching, through the iron-sharpening-iron interaction with others within His church—is uniquely able to make us aware when our lives are not matching up with the realities of our salvation. And in order to keep moving us in that direction, He will keep producing in us the accompanying fruit of repentance.

That's how we know we're His.

By our repentance.

It's the living fruit of redemption.

But obviously, this is where it gets tricky—and here's where some of our doubts can start rolling in—because we probably know by now that we're pretty good at faking repentance when we need to. We can be sorry and not *really* sorry, all at the same time. And so if the fruit of faith is repentance, and if our only way to change what's wrong with us is through trusting Jesus, then how can we tell if our repentance is real—the kind that truly leads to change?

That's what the rest of this chapter is all about.

Sin and Sorrow

Okay, so you're once again in that all too familiar place of discouragement and defeat—equal parts of anger, guilt, shame, and sadness. Condemning voices compound the intensity of it all. Your soul is screaming for a way out of this bondage. You're frustrated, perhaps to the point of despondency, giving up. You're a *lot* of things. And none of them are happy.

You feel really, really terrible about this.

The Bible, in 2 Corinthians 7:10, calls this terrible feeling "grief"—which is a word we more commonly apply to those times when someone has died, when we've lost a person we loved who was near to us. But *grief* is also a fitting term for describing what happens in the aftermath of sin. Of all the things our sin leaves us with, one of the worst is this: a measure of loss.

It may not be immediately recognizable perhaps. But at some point, in some way, we'll realize we've lost or are losing something as a result of this toxic combination of foolishness, poor judgment, and lack of self-control. We've lost time. We've lost hope. We've lost peace of mind or someone's trust. We've lost a two-month streak of sobriety, our self-respect, a lot of our old confidence, or maybe just whatever was left over from what was supposed to be an enjoyable weekend. Something. And even if we don't show it on our faces or let anybody else know it, we ourselves will know inside that we're grieving what it's cost us.

This is simply one of the built-ins of life on a fallen planet. We don't get a choice about whether or not sin will eventually result in a grief response. Ultimately, we will end up feeling some level of sorrow because of it.

But not all sorrow is the same.

Not all repentance is reflective of the gospel.

The Bible, again in 1 Corinthians 7, distinguishes between these various shades of sadness, dividing them into one of two broad categories: *godly grief* or *worldly grief.* The reactions of ours that fall into the first group lead us toward a life "without regret," which (we think we'd all agree) sounds pretty awesome. But the other ways of responding to our sin lead toward "death"—toward no kind of life at all.

Let's start by identifying some grief responses that are undoubtedly death-inducing—the kind we need to quit falling for:

Horizontal grief

Not too worried about what we did or who was affected, just really sorry we got caught. And if we *hadn't* gotten caught, we'd probably still be doing it. And if we can do it again *without* getting caught, that's probably what we're going to do next . . . more carefully this time.

This is the kind of sinful sorrow that responds to little more than our own pain. All we know is that our wife is angry, or our boss has called us into his office, or the bill is coming due, or the blue lights just snapped on behind us.

Could there be some weepy promises and "I'm sorrys" coming out of these events? Sure. Very possible. But tissues and teardrops don't tell the whole story. What's often missing from this picture is any view of God—a vertical reaction—the understanding that sin is bad not only because of how it stings but because of the poison it's made of. Horizontal grief is much less concerned about being broken, and much more upset about being busted.

Emotional grief

Again, all the crying and carrying on can make for some dramatic, sincere-sounding confessions. But raw emotion alone does not equal repentance. That's because emotions are truly the bouncy-houses of the human organism. They go up, they come down. Roll out, roll around. Can't walk a straight line or keep their balance for more than a few minutes. So once the show's over and the aspirin has started to kick in, those energized feelings—the ones that had you promising all those heartfelt "never-agains"—won't be anywhere to be found, no matter how much you seemed to mean it when you said it.

Whenever the main driver of recovery is emotional zeal alone, the fuel will always burn up once the passion has played out. The difference between changing our ways and being stuck in the same old stuff is often the same difference between wanting to be whole and just wanting to feel better again.

Passive grief

It's like the guy one of us saw on television recently who was showing off his pet lion. As in, "king of the jungle" lion. Fellow was leading it around on a chain like a dog. But during part of the taping, the cameras caught this enormous cat taking a swipe at the man's girlfriend. Mauled her. Came way close to killing her.

And amazingly, nobody could believe it.

We're talking about a lion here, okay? Attacking. Like the apex predator it is. And people standing around flabbergasted, wondering how a thing like this could happen.

Bad lion! Stop it!

You sit! You stay!

But that's what we sometimes want to believe about our sin. We're sad at how it's hurt us, or how it's caused us to hurt someone we care about. But, come on now, it's not nearly as ferocious as everybody says. If we just watch it more carefully, we can keep it under control. No problem. Won't happen again. If we just manage it a little better, we'll be fine. No need to overreact.

But sin can't be trained; sin must be killed. It won't ever just wet on the paper; it'll always end up trashing the whole house. The only way to change it is to get rid of it, not go around cleaning up after it or trying to teach it how to mind you. Sorrow comes from treating sin lightly; change comes from taking sin seriously.

Misplaced grief

This is another "worldly grief" reaction. You're upset that your sin happened, of course. You're not saying you did the right thing. But none of this would've happened *at all* (you think) if your spouse didn't spend so much money, if your kids hadn't gone over into the neighbor's yard, if your job wasn't so incessantly stressful, if your parents hadn't been so overbearingly Amish.

Listen, bottom line, nobody can make you *do* but you. Other people and outside situations can certainly press down hard on you, exerting some serious influence. But you're the one ultimately responsible for thinking your thoughts and choosing your actions.

Worldly grief, however, doesn't operate that way. It would much rather do the easy lifting of personal blame-shifting, even if it often disguises itself behind diplomatic apologies like, "I'm sorry if I offended you" or "If there's anything at all that I've done . . ."

Sure. Why accept the consequences of your own sin when you can dump it off on somebody else? Why go to the trouble of looking deeply at what you've done when it's so much easier just to fault somebody else for how they took it? Why take responsibility for your actions when there are so many other places it can go and still keep your conscience all warm and cozy? Call it what you want, but shared grief is just pride with a sad face. And it's worldly. It kills us.

Important to recognize that these past four actions (and others like them) are not exclusive to non-Christians. Even as believers, we can easily leak over into being "worldly" with our grief, just as we can be worldly in all kinds of other areas. But here's the thing: Only Christians have the available option of "grieving" in a way that brings about true, lasting change. Only the gospel can keep us from needlessly spinning our wheels, wasting valuable sweat and energy in a continually losing cause. Only as redeemed souls do we carry around inside ourselves any genuine hope and opportunity for regret-free living. For unlike the rest of humanity, Christians are not confined to grief responses that can never do anything but make us die a little more each day: trying so hard to act like we're not sinners, or to act like our sin is not really that big a deal—at least not as bad as it seems when we're the most bummed out about it.

But, yes, it is.

It's bad. Majorly bad.

And the sooner we realize this, the sooner we can start experiencing renewed confidence in our relationship with Christ, even in our need to repent for our sins and to plead for His help in strengthening our soft spots. Because as believers in Him, that's exactly what's supposed to happen. And because of His gospel, it's what can actually (finally) happen.

Repentance is not just the beginner course; repentance is lifetime learning. The goal of Christian living is not to get past the point of needing to repent, but to realize that God has made us capable through Christ of doing repentance well—repentance that the Bible calls "godly" in nature—what the apostle Paul described as "repentance leading to a knowledge of the truth" (2 Tim. 2:25)—repentance that leads to real change. At the root level. Where it can grow us up into character and consistency and confidence in Jesus' power and strength, fully at work in our pitiful weakness.

That's not shame and loss. Bad Christian.

That's mercy and grace. From a good, redeeming God.

Good Grief

So if sorrow is the sure result from our unavoidable brushes with sin and bad attitudes, let's promise we won't waste any more time on these stupid, old reactions that will never result in any significant change or succeed at anything other than killing our souls and continuing to harm the people around us. Let's choose instead, rather than feeling the need to look so invincible, pretending to be people we're not—or rather than giving up on ourselves altogether, thinking how disappointed God must be in us—let's finally start taking some redeemed alternatives for dealing with the reality of our stubborn, resistant, susceptible flesh. What if we knew that the grief we feel over the sin and weakness that still exist in our lives could actually be godly and gospel-inspired?

Here are several biblical ways of looking at it.[1]

I. Godly grief has clear vision.

Worldly grief, of course, is an old pro at downplaying and self-deception. But even though seeing our sin in all its horror can be a really painful thing to watch, may we never overlook the divine mercy involved when God strips off the blinders from our rationales and justifications and gives us the clarity to recognize exactly what we're doing.

In fact, the Bible says it's the *wicked* person who "flatters himself too much to discover and hate his sin" (Ps. 36:2 HCSB). It was the prodigal *son,* however—the one who had strayed from his father yet remained a rightful heir by virtue of their family relationship—who "came to himself" in the pigsty and realized he had sinned not only against his father but also "against heaven" (Luke 15:17–18).

The Word of God will do that for us. It's surgical. It cuts. It reveals. It opens up our insides, right out there on the MRI slab. And doesn't miss one ugly detail in the process. Everything comes to light and into view.

But don't you ever dare despise that—because He doesn't do it to shame us; He does it to redeem us. This is firsthand evidence, not of God's damning condemnation, but His precious grace, taking the careful initiative to pinpoint the places where we're sick and diseased, so that He can show us exactly what we need of Him and how He can make us whole.

If you ever feel the Scriptures pinning your back to the seat when you're listening in church, or praying at home, or reading on the commuter train, do not turn away or try switching the station, avoiding the exposure. No. Hear it. Absorb it. Receive it. Own it. Then offer it up to Him in repentance. Your Redeemer, the only one who can restore you, is there to root it out of you.

2. Godly grief produces sorrow.

When people in the Scriptures recognized just how ghastly their sins were—when God opened their eyes wide enough for them to finally *see* it—they were appalled, horrified, grief-stricken. They felt the "embitterment" of soul that's wrapped up in the meaning of "godly grief," defined in the Bible as our proper response to sin.

And perhaps none of these individuals was more notable than the woman—the prostitute—who slipped up behind Jesus during a get-together at the home of a Pharisee, weeping, then knelt down to anoint His feet with expensive ointment, wiping away the tears with her hair. The smug and self-righteous men who were standing around, fully aware of this woman's reputation and profession, couldn't believe what a spectacle she was causing, couldn't believe what Jesus was allowing to go on at such a fine person's home at such a fine social gathering. But all this girl knew—and all she could see—was that she was a "sinner" (Luke 7:37). The sight of her failings became the grief of her heart.

And as soon as we're struck by the same vision of ourselves, that's when our first response can be the same as hers—faith, full release, sorrow, worship—knowing that His response will be the same as well: "Your sins are forgiven. . . . Your faith has saved you . . . go in peace."

3. Godly grief readily confesses.

After *seeing* your sin, and *sorrowing* over your sin, the worst thing you can do is to try *stuffing* your sin, hoping nobody ever finds out who you really are. Turns out, the best way to avoid being found out a fake is just not to be one—to be open with people about your struggles, while being equally as open in your praise of God for what He's making of you, despite your many messes and problems.

This is where the church comes in so beautifully, because it gets us around people who can help us carry the nagging issues of our hearts—people to whom we can confess our battles with sin and confess our need for a Savior—while we're doing the same for them. When the only person that truly knows all about us is the person who uses our hairbrush, we are easy pickings for the Enemy, ripe for being outmaneuvered and outsmarted. That's how we remain slaves to our repeated failures, by basically resisting the redeeming love of God and the needed, encouraging support of others. Because even if we're as much as 99 percent known (or much less, as is more often the case) to our spouse, our friends, our family, and the people around us, we are still not fully known. We're still hiding out. We're still covering up.

We don't want them to know *everything*.

But true sorrow over sin begs to be vented—both vertically to God and horizontally to others. So mark this down: You have no shot at experiencing real change in life if you're habitually protecting your image, hyping your spiritual brand, and putting out the vibe that you're a lot more unfazed by temptation than the reality you know and live would suggest. Even Satan himself cannot succeed at clobbering you with condemnation when the stuff he's accusing you of doing is the same stuff you've been honestly admitting before God and others and trusting the Lord for His help with. That's some of the best action you can take against the sin in your life. That's responsible repentance.

4. Godly grief causes us to blush.

"See what earnestness this godly grief has produced in you," Paul said in 2 Corinthians 7:11, "what eagerness to clear your-selves, what indignation." Yes, if allowed to turn into shame, your frustration with yourself—this "indignation"—can contort into a death spiral, ironically leading you to repeat the same destructive behavior that sent you tumbling to begin with. It can trick you into slinking away toward food, drugs, laziness, pornography (or whatever), to get your mind off how rotten you feel for abusing food or drugs or being lazy or looking at pornography. It's crazy.

It's deadly.

But in the hands of our Redeemer, the red face of indignation is able to defy the laws of shame and gravity. Instead of sinking us even lower into our sin and into ourselves, it propels us forward, stuns us back to sensibility, and points up by contrast with our disappointing counterfeits the beauties of what we've been missing and of what we now most desire.

Yes, sin can lead to the slouched shoulders, the long face, the head hanging down in defeat and disbelief. But the Lord, according to David the psalmist, is known as the "lifter" of our head (Ps. 3:3), placing His hand under our chin, raising our gaze to meet His, and gently calling us back—calling us up—toward the life He meant for us all along.

In the end, godly grief produces within us such a *hatred* of our sin, we then receive from God the renewed motivation to actually *turn* from our sin. This doesn't mean we'll be never again be drawn toward it, that under the right combination of moods and scenarios we won't ever feel wistfully deserving of it, fidgety for it. But when Hebrews 12:2 says Jesus went to the cross "despising the shame," part of what He was scorning, detesting, and being driven by—grimacing through the pain, intent on killing it—was the shame He knew we'd suffer from being addicted to substitute gods. He hates what they make us feel, hates what they make us think. And by His death, He's made a way for us to fight back and attack them, to overcome them, to turn away from them . . . to want those lions dead.

And the more of them we let Him slay for us, refusing to keep them around in case we might need them later, the more often we can actually start cranking that repentance wheel back counterclockwise. Rather than always needing to deal with sin's aftertaste—the injury and pain, the humiliating loss—we can more frequently anticipate its fallout ahead of time, turning to God in obedience and surrender, even while temptation is still doing its warm-up act. We can give in to God instead of our appetites. Relinquish our clingy need for control and comfort. Lay down our fears of loneliness or rejection. Cast our cares on the Lord and see if that doesn't end up feeling a whole lot better the next morning.

But either way, the fruit of turning to God—*before* we sin, *after* we've sinned, even right there in the *middle* of our sin—is where Christians go to experience the flavors of God-fearing honor, gratitude, dependence, worship, confidence, trust, freedom, revival. Even those sins from our past that have been the most regrettable, the most difficult to move beyond—the ones we'd give anything if we could go back and do over again—Christ is able to redeem and rewrite even those into masterful sequels and come-from-behind victories. He takes what's given us fits for so long and gives us instead a reason to celebrate what He's done.

To celebrate our redemption. To celebrate our Redeemer.

So if perhaps you've been thinking your job is to keep God impressed, or if you've grown so sick of what you've turned out to be that you've almost given up hope of ever trying to change this person anymore, realize there is "more joy in heaven over one sinner who repents than over ninety-nine righteous persons who need [or who *think* they need] no repentance" (Luke 15:7).

Yes, even the struggle is something to celebrate.

Chapter 5

The Benefits of Belief

Justification and Adoption

"Repent and *believe*," Jesus said. Any proper treatment of the gospel must include "belief" as a key part of the discussion—both what it is and what it isn't. Well-meaning people can hold a number of different biblical interpretations on how redemption works, who does what, what happens when, the way it's eternally transacted. But somewhere within any orthodox understanding of Christ and the gospel is this vitally important element: the authentic flow of belief from redeemed to Redeemer.

"Believe in the Lord Jesus, and you will be saved" (Acts 16:31). Can't get much clearer than that.

And yet the deeper we go into what salvation entails and what it means, and the more we actually begin infusing its promises and benefits into every extremity of our lives—from fingertip to pinky toe—something remarkable happens to our belief. We're not talking, now, about people who treat Christianity as an add-on, who stick it into their wallet along with all the other cards and IDs they carry. To people like that, the gospel is sure to stay sounding fairly benign and routine. Uninteresting. Mostly decaf. Highly forced and forgettable. Wedged into tight scheduling blocks around the kids' soccer practice and piano lessons. If it weren't for Christmas Eve coming along every year to pump up the excitement a little, their faith might sail right into February without ever teasing out much more than a few blinks of their focus or face time.

But when people stop pushing their Christian faith into the margins, stop saving it for later, stop taking it in such small doses . . .

When they quit acting as if they are the sovereign ruler of their own lives, calling all the shots, deigning to toss God a few devotional minutes every now and then, if they're not too sleepy at night . . .

When their relationship with Him becomes what truly drives and determines everything else, then they begin to make an amazing discovery about the claims of the gospel. They start to realize that it's more than just something to believe. It's actually, in more ways than they can count . . .

Unbelievable.

That's how the gospel finally struck Adam. He'd attended church fairly regularly as a kid. But with his family constantly boiling in crisis and chaos, with his parents' marriage teetering on divorce most of the time, the fake niceness and platitudes of Sunday morning always struck him as sort of an alternate universe, oddly out of phase with what was actually happening out there under people's shade trees and rooftops. So after finally attaining enough age and freedom and the option of making his own choices, Adam ultimately threw himself into band gigs and philosophical study and the heady arguments of agnosticism, find-ing these to be a much better fit for squaring up the real life he saw around him. Or at least felt more honest.

That didn't mean he was any happier, of course. By the time the gospel got through to him, he had picked up some drug habits, a porn problem, a daily struggle with anxiety and depression, was living with his girlfriend in New York City, and had lost all hope that God (or anybody) could possibly love someone who was so guilt-ridden and despicable.

But slowly, and surely, in the brighter days that followed, the "unbelievable" truths of redemption began to settle deeper and deeper into his soul. Not only did God love him; He loved him at his worst. And He was offering Adam a way of escape—through repen-tance—into a life that didn't only *sound* confident when laid out in Scripture, but actually *felt* confident when trotted out into the day.

The first thing he did was confess his porn addiction to Heather, his girlfriend, and get into recovery with other Christians who could help him turn his renewed passion for purity into a lifestyle. Heather wasn't a believer, didn't really understand what all this meant, but was glad to see him working hard to get over something that wasn't good for him, for her, for them.

But one day he came home and told her something else: that they needed to stop sleeping together. God's Word had been convicting him that their sexual relationship was outside the boundaries of right and wrong. Not only that, but he'd come to the conclusion over time that he was making a mockery of God's purposes for marriage, that unless they were both in covenant with Him as well as in covenant with each other, their relationship couldn't continue and be pleasing to the Lord.

This wasn't a legalistic play. He simply wanted to experience more and more of God, following through on his rekindled desire to be obedient, to follow. And he wanted more for Heather as well—didn't want her tied in with somebody who was living a double life, who was leading her into sin, who said with his words that he loved her but didn't really care about what was ultimately best for her.

He was torn and crying by this time, by this part of the conversation—wanting God, wanting Heather, wanting marriage, but feeling that their relationship would need to change so dramatically, she might not be willing to agree to it. He was sure she wasn't going to put up with these kinds of demands just because his life had been changed by this wild idea that a God was out there who loved him, who'd died for him, who'd forgiven him and was turning him into somebody totally new and different. He was certain this rapid, slingshot turn of events was going to be more than she could handle. No more sex. No more apartment. No more of what they'd seen and done and been and loved.

Unbelievable, what was happening.

Yes.

Just unbelievable enough for Heather to believe it too.

They sat there on the floor together—no temper, no crash of bags being packed, no raised voices and slamming doors. Instead she took his hands into hers, looked deeply into his eyes, and said, "If you want God that much, Adam . . . then I want Him too."

Unbelievable.

What God does for us through redemption—working through the cooperation of our belief—is simply hard to believe. Unreal. Incredible. How He loves us. How He changes us.

And all we want to do in this chapter is just take a couple of these gospel principles, unpack them from the gift box for you, and place them right here in your lap where you can take them out, feel the weight, spin them around in your hands, and see them from all sides.

These two biblical truths, which start out as the solid ground under your spiritual feet, are what unbelievably come together to form the trampoline of change.

Justification

Justification is a legal term—which, judging from the number of *CSI* and *NCIS* shows that have dominated television since the early 2000s, should put it at least within the field of play for us to understand it.

Modern culture is enamored with law and justice. Put a bimbo on trial today for killing her lover, and it'll make the coverage of the Kennedy assassination look like grocery store commercials. There'll be six talking heads on screen, each of them arguing over the top of the other, all at the same time, dissecting every eye blink and facial expression of the accused in the courtroom.

We love the big cases, love the investigative reporting, the kind where some government official is chased by a photojournalist through the parking lot, camera jostling, refusing to answer questions about his part in an alleged cover-up or a damning set of personal charges. And we love seeing the bad guys, whether on the big screen or the local news, rounded up and put away.

That's because we are a people who understand law. We want fairness. We want the truth to come out. We want the offended to be cleared and for somebody to pay.

We want *justice*.

And guess what—the gospel gives it to us.

In the most unbelievable way of all.

The biblical idea of justification basically means that the gavel has banged down, and we've been totally pardoned—declared *innocent*—which, at first blush, while sounding way too good to be true, sounds also like the judicial joke of the century. We thought God was everywhere all the time, that nothing escaped His all-seeing notice, that even those things we did in the dark were being filmed for later broadcast when all would come into the light. How in the *world*, then—based on the preponderance of evidence that could be displayed against us—could we get off with a not-guilty verdict? Did we just get in His blind spot somehow? Have we slipped through on a technicality or something?

The secret, of course—the mystery—is that the Judge has rendered His decision based not on what *we've* done, on *our* innocence (since "by works of the law no one will be justified"—Gal. 2:16), but on the sacrifice and willing substitution of the innocent, crucified Christ. We are still lawbreakers. And we keep at it, even in trying to fight it, even on this side of our belief and salvation. But the "good news" is that Jesus has come to us, God in flesh, and has drunk the full winepress of wrath that our sins deserve. As a result—unbelievably—God has imputed to us (credited to us, ascribed to us, placed into our account) all the innocence and righteousness and perfection of Christ.

Therefore, a miserable end to our lives has been miraculously averted. Not in theory or through the roundabout logic of seminary lecture. Not by spiritual delusion or false hopes. Not on the condition that we cross our fingers and be really careful from here on out. No—none of that. His resurrection (as if His crucifixion weren't enough) provides all the objective evidence we need that proves His promises are true, that His ability to conquer death is real, and that His atonement for our sin is actively in force.

We have been *justified* before God. Pardoned and ascribed righteousness. Book it. An unbelievable brand of gospel justice has been served . . . and is undeserved.

But wait. There's more.

New Identity

Listen to most people's Christian testimonies, or dig into your own heart, and the majority of us would say we've come around to grasping at least the concept that, okay, God has chosen for some divine reason to forgive our sins. We can see the cross. We know what it represents. We understand we don't deserve it, but we accept it. We love it. And we love Him for doing it.

For justifying us.

For seeing us as pure and blameless.

But the moment we were justified, something else was taking place simultaneously. Justification-plus. Both of these things were accomplished in a moment's time. Snap, snap. Couldn't tell their timing apart. But from an experiential standpoint—the way it feels, the way we live it—most of us, at the cost of a lot of joy and relief and freedom and blessing, typically take years, sometimes *many* years, maybe *all* our years before we can wrap our heads and hearts around this one other aspect of the gospel's benefit package.

Romans 8:15–17 defines it like this:

- that we have received "the Spirit of *adoption*"

- that we are now "children of God"
- and "if children, then heirs"
- we are "fellow heirs with Christ"

Both of us (Matt, Michael) are dads. We've each held our newborn children in our arms. And in those moments, we realized that these precious children were worth giving our lives for (or taking another's) in order to protect.

Think of it: those children hadn't done anything for us when we first held them, when we first loved them. In fact, up until that time, they'd only been trouble for us—most especially, of course, for our wives—but for us too, by virtue of our close proximity to the situation. They'd already cost us sleep. (And they would cost us more.) They'd already cost us money. (They would cost us much, much more.) They'd already eaten up Saturdays and weeknights, times when we might've wanted to do something else, but there were things to go buy for the baby, there were closets to clean out for the baby, there was furniture that needed assembling for the baby. These little guys hadn't even spoken a word yet, hadn't colored us one picture, hadn't made an A on any report card, hadn't wrapped up a single pair of Father's Day socks.

And we *loved* them. Already.

They were ours. They were special.

They brought us to tears of pure joy.

But both of us as dads could look at each other right now, even after our many years of parenting, and feel the same thing that you're probably feeling. We still have a hard time believing that God our Father could love us and feel for us the same joy and pride and protectiveness and willingness that we have for our kids. *More*, in fact.

It's unbelievable.

God has not just given us a break; He's given us identity.

He is not only our Judge; He's our Father.

And maybe for you, that idea doesn't naturally come across as comforting news, the way it might immediately seem to others. Your story may be more like Clarissa's, who grew up in a fatherless home from the age of two. Didn't even meet her father until she was in the seventh grade, after reaching out trying to contact him herself. Soon she began corresponding with him, got to know him, saw what he looked like, saw how much of herself was actually a part of him—his face, his hands, his gestures and mannerisms. It was so wonderful, felt so completing, for the first time in her life to be the daughter of a real-live dad.

But six months after their first meeting, just as she was going into the eighth grade, Clarissa received a letter from her father, saying he'd made a mistake in agreeing to pursue a relationship with her. This just wasn't going to work. He had other things to do, other obligations to keep, and she was a complication to all of it. He didn't know what he'd expected when he hesitantly consented to visit with her, but at this point, she needed to know what to expect going forward. He didn't want any further contact with her. Of any kind.

Goodbye, Clarissa.

Forever.

You know how kids are. They dream. They imagine. They still allow themselves room to hope. Clarissa had always thought this man—this legend of a man, her father—would one day ride into her world on his white horse and rescue her from a half-empty life. But now, he'd ridden right by. There was no fairy tale to live, no prince for this princess. And with the curtain pulled down on what might have been happiness ever after, her life began to darken even further into nightmare. Rage, hate, brokenness, self-destruction. Drugs, dropout, pregnancy, suicide—or at least something very close to it.

But what she learned as a redeemed young woman—what God will help all of us to learn, if we'll let Him, if we'll believe—is that He is the father our own father would've been if not for the sin that messed him up . . . the sin that messes all of us up. God has entered our lives to *redeem* us, even from good dads, faithful dads, who did their best but even in loving us could not love the way our Father loves.

The way He loves *you,* if you're His child.

That is your identity—a son, a daughter of God, the heavenly King, the Ruler over all, Judge of the whole earth. And because He can, and because He chooses, He is also Father . . . Father to His children.

And if you don't know this, or if you still can't believe it—or can't act on it or allow yourself to feel it—He has provided a way to communicate this truth to you where you can understand it deep inside, no matter how rejected you've been. No matter how disillusioned. No matter how betrayed or mistreated.

He has not only given you a new identity, He has given you His Spirit. And this Spirit of adoption "bears witness" that we are the "children of God" (Rom. 8:16).

Part of the Family

The person who pounded through a two-mile run this morning, or lifted some weights, or played three games of racquetball, then ate a banana and a bran muffin for breakfast on their way out—they're probably feeling pretty good about themselves today, about the condition of their physical body . . . or at least feel good about the direction they're heading.

Why?

Because their workout and diet experience this morning—perhaps on a lot of mornings—*bears witness* to their identity as someone who values (or is learning to value) good stewardship of their bodies, who places a priority on improving and maintaining their health and fitness.

But what about the person who rarely if ever tries to eat right, or exercise, or take the stairs—and doesn't really have any desire to be any different? What if he's actually a bit derogatory toward those who go to the gym and count calories and drink water all day? What if she makes fun of people who ask for a doggie bag at lunch so they can take home the other half for supper that night? What is there to *testify* to the idea that this person cares about his or her overall well-being or places much stock in any part of the whole notion?

A lot of times, the reason we struggle to feel and receive the love of God—to see ourselves as His beloved, adopted children—is because we're not pursuing in our everyday lives those things His Word describes as being valuable and significant. We're not showing respect or esteem for those qualities that would cause us to reflect the character of Christ, that give us a family resemblance. And because our spirit is looking the other way from where God's

Spirit is drawing us—from those places where He knows we'll find delight and confidence and settledness and fulfillment—then why should we expect our lives to mesh with His Spirit's testimony? How would we ever begin to feel like one of His kids if in our hearts we don't really want to be?

None of us would dare to say, of course, that we follow Him perfectly. We'll never be flawless in the execution. Repentance, you'll recall, is a key component of living out the gospel. But is the desire there? Do we want it? Is our heart leaning in the direction of obedience and trust? If we could only get our stubborn will to line up with our wishes on a reliable basis, isn't that the way we'd want to go? Isn't that why we fight ourselves so hard?

"The righteous falls seven times," the Bible says—which tells us that Christians are certainly not above experiencing the occasional face plant, sometimes one right after another. The difference, however, is that the son or daughter of God "rises again" (Prov. 24:16), even on scraped hands and scuffed knees. We may only be crawling by that point, barely getting back to our feet. But our eyes are pointing forward, and our intent is to press on, "looking to Jesus, the founder and perfecter of our faith" (Heb. 12:2).

And the more consistently this happens—this again-and-again pursuit of Him—the more clearly the Spirit will bear witness "with our spirit" that we truly do belong to Him, that we are indeed the children of God.

Try it and see.

Now if no desire is present—no interest in following God, no respect for Him as Father, no real inclination to do what He says—then, yes, it's fair to question whether you've actually trusted Him for salvation. Because (watch out: hard truth coming up here) *He's not everybody's Father.* We're not all His children. Sorry to disappoint the Olympics Committee and the people who like to mention His name in their Emmy Award acceptance speeches. The family of God is big, but it's not universal. He's everyone's *Creator*—roger that—but He's only *Father* to those who've been redeemed through His gospel, those whom He's adopted by grace into this uniquely tender, eternal, unalterable family relationship.

And so when you sense the desire to obey your Father, when you set your face again toward doing His will—even after a season of missing it badly, seriously doubting His trustworthiness—that's the Spirit of adoption you're feeling, pulling you up close, listening to where you hurt, being honest enough to tell you the hard truth, yet smiling His grace and encouragement, then giving you a gentle, loving push back into the pursuit . . . and watching to be sure you're okay out there.

Because this pursuit is taking us someplace incredible. *Unbelievable.* And He knows it. Our Father God one day is going to remake all creation. He's going to restore the peaceful, worry-free contentment that existed before sin ever entered the world. He's going to give us resurrected bodies that never run down, never wear out, never go over the hill, and never forget and leave our shopping list behind at home on the kitchen counter. Won't be needing any Botox or rinses or mammograms or prostate screenings. No heartburn relief, no Icy Hot, no reading glasses, not even any breath mints.

And better still—better even than giving us the body we've always wanted, living in a place more beautiful and perfect than we can possibly imagine—He's going to give us *Himself.* We'll be able to enjoy unbroken, unending, visible access with our strong

"Abba Father," which is a million times more precious and desirable than all His other blessings put together.

That's the inheritance being stored up and waiting for His kids—for His heirs, heirs of God. And that's the very identity the gospel ascribes to us—as fellow heirs with Christ—"provided we suffer with him in order that we may also be glorified with him" (Rom. 8:17).

Ooh. Wait. Back up there a second. "Suffer with him?" This was all sounding really great up till then. Loving this justified/adopted thing we've been talking about. Feeling really good about that. But what's this suffering business have to do with it? Not so sure this deal is so unbelievable after all.

Oh, but yes, it is.

Look, we should be glad the Bible doesn't dodge around the grimy, sweaty, painful realities of life on this fractured planet. God's Word is honest. He always tells the truth. And so, yes, even His children must deal with some hard memories from their past and with fresh challenges in their present and future. None of us is spared from feeling loss and soreness and sadness and misunderstanding, the same way our own kids must face these things in the world. In fact, the call to follow Jesus Christ, rather than being a ticket *away* from suffering, is actually a doorway straight *into* it—just as His own calling on earth was marked by difficulty and resistance, by pain and hardship.

This is what sin has done to our life down here.

This is its brutal legacy on display.

But far from being a tarnish on the otherwise unbelievable things of God, these dark nights of the soul become times when He draws us even more securely to Him, when His Spirit testifies to us even more confidently of the Father's love and steadfastness. The reason He can tell us to "count it all joy" when we meet "trials of various kinds" (James 1:2)—which pretty much covers it all, wouldn't you say?—is because He does some of His best work amid our worst pain. Our senses are never more awakened to our need for His love than when our need is most exposed. He is not the author of this evil and suffering, but He knows how to turn the blackest typeface into something richly colorful and redemptive for His children.

He is our Father, who will never forsake or abandon us, who loves us and has given us His name, who has bestowed on us a new identity in Christ—and who also happens to be our Judge, yet has declared us totally innocent and free through the just, atoning sacrifice of the Lord Jesus on our behalf.

So we are justified before the law bench of heaven.

We've been adopted into His heavenly family.

And because of these two all-consuming realities, all the ingredients are in place for us to deal strongly and confidently with whatever comes our way, including those many sins of ours that have been so adept at defeating us for so long. The way has been cleared for us to square up and stand tall.

Now's our chance to just go out there and live it.

To watch Him watching over us.

And to watch us change.

Chapter 6

Turn Here

The Navigation of Sanctification

Imagine you've relocated to a new house or apartment in another neighborhood. It's actually not that far from the place where you lived before. To get there, you still go down some of the same roads, past some of the same scenery and landmarks. But now, when you're coming home from work or from church or a party at your best friend's house, and you reach this one particular intersection . . .

Instead of turning left, you turn right.

The first few weeks, this new change of direction felt very strange and unnatural. You'd made a left at that traffic light so many times, for so long, sheer force of habit would kick in. Sometimes if your mind was distracted, if you were sort of auto-piloting or not paying close enough attention, you might catch yourself peeling over to the left, like always, queuing up into the turn lane, or even sailing a few blocks down the street before you'd look up and recognize your mistake. *(Oh! I forgot.)* But for a little while, every time you pulled up to that spot, the decision of which way to turn required a cognitive act of the will to remember what to do. You had to intentionally tell yourself, against the familiar tug of your old pattern and reflex—"Be sure to hang a right up here."

Because you'd changed addresses.

You didn't live down that other way anymore.

There's a key aspect of the gospel that's captured in this simplistic analogy, in terms of how the Holy Spirit builds it out in our lives through the years. When Christ captured your heart with His grace and mercy, remember, you were immediately *justified*, declared innocent in the most supreme of all Supreme Courts. At the same time, you were also *adopted*, which put you on the list of God's personal dependents, loved like the child of the King you instantly became. Between these two incredible changes to your status and stability, your spiritual position before God became anchored in ten full trucks of concrete—which means if there's anything you should know for sure in life, it's this: you can never be chiseled out and hauled off from the place where He's put you. Not by *anybody*, not by *anything*. You're planted. Deep. Solid as a rock. In Jesus.

But your heavenly Father isn't satisfied just knowing that your foundations and future are eternally secure. What He's after— what He knows in His infinite wisdom is the most satisfying burst of joy and fresh air that His kids can ever experience on earth—is the growing reality of a holy, transformed, right-turning life. Not just *positional* holiness, but *manifest* holiness. Friday afternoon at 5:00 holiness. Hanging out with your friends holiness. All by yourself at home holiness. Everywhere you are. Holiness.

And we've got some good news for you: the gospel covers this, as well.

But unlike the instantaneous gifts of justification and adoption, which are deposited in full all at once into our account, this additional gospel perk is more of a process, not a pronouncement.

Think of it in terms of the children of Israel. Think back to the part of their history that occurs from Exodus all the way into the first chapters of Joshua. Through the miraculous sovereignty of God, working through the Israelites' faith in the sprinkled blood of Passover, the Lord sprung them free from slavery with one mighty wave of deliverance. He orchestrated His will through Moses, the plagues, the parting of the Red Sea, the folding up of Pharaoh—and before you knew it, God's people were leaving behind four long centuries of captivity in the blazing hot sands of Egypt.

But their next stop wasn't the Promised Land; it was the wilderness—forty years of testing, trial, and growth—designed to show them "what was in [their] heart" (Deut. 8:2), designed to show them what was in His loving, guiding hand. And we, too, can expect the same progression to occur in our own lives. From Egypt to Canaan. From conversion to heaven. And all points in between.

That's where *sanctification* takes place—another great gospel word to recover.

Sanctification is reserved only for God's justified, adopted children. Because without Christ, without the gospel, all we can ever expect to do, even in doing out best, is to run full speed ahead down the wrong, dead-end path. (How depressing.) But *with* Him—with His love constantly drawing us toward change and redemption—we can actually begin to experience in our daily traffic patterns what His grace has already accomplished in us for all eternity. The shafts of light and hope that emanate from way out there on the horizon can be warming up the car in our driveway this very morning, getting us ready to head out onto paths of righteousness for the rest of the day.

And so the promise of sanctification is able to turn what may feel like a test today, like a trial by fire—like way more temptation or trouble than we can handle—into a muscle-building exercise that strengthens our spiritual core. It's the gospel, still on the job, repeatedly reassuring us as we submit to the Father's driving directions that our confidence is well placed in His love, wisdom, protection, and blessing.

So sanctification isn't something we lean back on, as much as it's something we lean into. Rather than being an action only God can do, all by Himself (the way justification and adoption are), sanctification is an endeavor He undertakes in full cooperation and partnership with us. It requires us to exert what you might call "grace-driven effort"—made possible only by the merciful initiative of God, of course, and yet fully employing our human brains, brawn, and body parts as we go.

Oh, and also our blinker.

Learning to turn right, where we used to turn wrong.

Life and Death

We're guessing, since you've hung in there with us this far, that your interest in "turning right" is pretty high on the wish list. You've found (as all of us do) that the decisions involved in changing course, despite how badly you may want their results on most days, are rarely easy. Especially at first. Going in God's direction doesn't just happen automatically. It takes work. Takes sacrifice. Takes truly believing that what you'll find at the other end is much better and more satisfying than what you always wind up dealing with by turning the other way.

But it's the life you've been dying for.

And that makes it worth the effort.

So without spending a whole lot more time on what sanctification is, what do you say we cut straight to the part about how sanctification works. And to get us started, let's head up to the big board—"Gospel Living for $800, Alex"—and deposit a couple of new (old) vocabulary terms into our functional word bank.

Sanctification is basically composed of these two elements: *vivification* and *mortification*.

What is . . . ?

Vivification

You probably haven't seen or used this word in a sentence lately—or *ever*—but it basically means to quicken or animate, to bring to life. *Vivid* would be a related word. Hi-def visuals, maybe. And according to Colossians 3, this is what starts to happen to us spiritually when we "seek" or "set our minds" on those things "that are above, not on things that are on the earth"—when we spend time marinating in the fact that our very souls, right this minute, are "hidden with Christ in God" (vv. 1–3).

The Bible says you've been given the authority to take your thoughts "captive" (2 Cor. 10:5), to monitor what you think about, so that instead of being "conformed to this world" with its wide selection of sin varieties and short-sighted values, your life can truly be "transformed by the renewal of your mind" (Rom. 12:2). Instead of believing lies, instead of nursing distortions, you can choose to dwell on the truths of the gospel, which you can be sure will always far transcend whatever's trending on social media this afternoon.

We're talking about thinking new stuff. True stuff. In the mind is where vivification begins to build its head of steam. By dwelling on what's eternally accurate about God and about ourselves, we are able to see that our lives are not uncontrolled and uncontrollable, impossible to be corralled, but rather can be brought into alignment with truth, so that we can make them do what we want them to do—what God has *created* them to do—for our good and His glory.

Vivification involves filling ourselves with a renewed way of thinking, based on ultimate realities—those things that stir up our love, gratitude, and affections for Jesus—while getting our minds *off* the nagging, noisy combination of sound bites, bad advice, rumors, old wives' tales, trivia, others' opinions, devilish accusations, breaking news, and all the unholy influences we allow to rattle around in our brains all day, from beer commercials and movie trailers to temporary worries and a whole carousel of covetous desires.

This is why the Word of God is so essential in the daily, ongoing life of a believer. Because from the minute you close your Bible in the morning, you're entering a world that's fighting every truth and teaching it represents. At every turn. And if God's message is not deep inside you, where you can meditate on it, return to it, and frequently call it back to mind, you won't be able to discern what's really true from what may be really intriguing, really alluring, really convincing, but really false. And really defeating.

Taking charge of your mind, making sure your thoughts are pointing toward and pursuing Jesus, is how you remember where your new house is—down *this* street, not *that* one—needing a *right* turn to get there, not a *left*.

Any one of a million thoughts can get you lost if you follow them out to their logical conclusions. But only the mind trained on Jesus will keep driving you home.

Mortification

If you can think of *vivification* as the life-giving plant food and fertilizer that you spade into your garden, *mortification* is the knuckle-busting process of pulling up the weeds. And you can't do one without the other. Because if all you're doing is water-blasting more Bible reading and sermon notes into your spiritual soil, but not actively clearing out the thick, thorny attitudes and behaviors that don't belong there, then you're just leaving the ground cluttered beyond capacity, draining out all its nutrients, and basically ensuring that you'll never be happy with what grows in it.

There are things that just need to be "put to death" in us (Col. 3:5), taken outside and popped in the head a couple of times. *Bang, bang.* We're not meaning to get too violent on you here, but when it comes to how we treat the invaders and violators that intrude on our spiritual freedom, our tendency is to be way too polite and accommodating with them . . . and to feel way too confident in our own ability to keep them from poking their heads back up through the ground.

The only healthy sin is dead sin. And the longer we put up with this junk in our lives—the longer we wait to kill the lion— then the longer it takes before we can pull up to that same inter- section, feel our eyes drawn in the direction where we used to live, and yet still make the right turn with confident ease, or at least with a steadier hand of trust, discipline, and determination.

Headed home.

The Bible, of course, is as important to mortification as it is to the V-word. The Scripture can help us outline a whole lot of things in our lives that are only good for being yanked up and burned in the backyard: "sexual immorality, impurity, passion [or lust], evil desire, and covetousness . . . anger, wrath, malice, slander, and obscene talk" (Col. 3:5, 8). Open and shut. Cut and dried. Black and white.

But you're also likely to find, as you keep maturing in the faith and growing deeper into the sanctification process, that God's Spirit will increasingly alert you to certain activities and environ- ments of yours, certain habits and hobbies, that—even though they're not morally wrong—are still personally detrimental to your own heart. And could stand to be euthanized.

There's no Bible verse, for example, that prohibits sleeping in till 10:00 on a Saturday, or purchasing a lottery ticket, or listening to music that reminds you of your wilder days, or buying two big bags of Cheetos when they're on a good sale price. But for what- ever reason—for you—there's just a noticeable drag on your zeal for Christ that slips in when you do these things, or watch these things, or play around with these things, or get in the vicinity of these things. You can feel a palpable drift toward self-gratification and compromise after you've gone there. Participating in it just always ignites some old feelings that compete with your purity and take the edge off your spiritual desire.

And so there's often wisdom in *mortifying* that particular distraction—whatever it is—in order to keep your heart *vivacious* in following hard after the Lord. It may seem weird to somebody else. They may think you're being overly introspective, taking your faith a little too far. But what's more valuable to you? Watching *Saturday Night Live*, or preparing your Saturday night heart for Sunday morning worship? Keeping those one or two websites in your usual rotation, or not ever being tempted to scroll down to the cheerleader pictures ever again?

Vivification. Mortification. They're quite literally a matter of life and death. They're what come together in God's training curriculum to help you transmit the gospel from the theological study right into your living room. They're the exercise equipment that keeps you pumped up about Jesus, while keeping you powered down on everything else that turns your eye away from Him.

Weed Treatments

But just like we're able to repent *well* or repent *poorly*, there are both effective ways and ineffective ways of navigating the test tracks of sanctification. Just as the short distance from Egypt to Canaan became for the ancient Israelites a round-and-round do-over that lasted an entire generation, we can grind the sanctification process to a snail's pace if we don't fully and willingly cooperate. God *is* patient, and He *will* keep working on us and with us. No need ever to doubt that. But we can drag this out and restrict ourselves from making much progress if we insist on doing it our own way.

One of the slowdowns that interferes with the pace of sanctification is what we call "mowing over" our sin, treating only the high-level symptoms, not drilling down deep to eradicate the roots that keep producing all these weeds and problems to start with. And as we've watched this shortcut occur over the years, we've found that the places where we're most likely to see it happening—to see the results of our shoddy landscaping—are in the fields of *relationships* and *addictions.*

Relationships

Okay, the sentence we're about to write is a real game changer, so get ready for it. We're thinking here in terms of relational conflict, relational strife. It could be with your spouse, your children, your in-laws, your supervisor, your brother or sister, your parents. Pick one, add another. But put in your mind right now a difficult relationship that's causing you some major headaches and anger, making you want to talk ugly into the windshield when you're out driving. Lots of internal wrestling and stubborn wills. Impossible people. You know the kind.

Are we tracking? You got it? Because here's the sentence . . .

The conflict you're having is not primarily about *them*; God is working in this conflict to reveal something about *you.*

The easiest thing to do when we start locking horns with another person is just to bail. Write them off. Don't answer their calls anymore. Go to a different church. Go find a new set of friends. Maybe even a new wife or husband. Renegotiate the terms of this relationship. On *our* terms. But in most cases, while we're digging our teeth into what this person or these people have done to hurt us and make life difficult for us, we're not seeing the need for digging up very much in our own part of the yard. We're becoming an expert in this other person's flaws and weaknesses, but hardly ever touching the ones that we're contributing ourselves, the ones that are coming out at high volume (if not in silent treatments) amid all the commotion.

If you want to know who you really are, watch what happens when you interact over time with other people. Because they'll show you. See what's revealed about yourself when you come into close contact with them. Why do single men and women suddenly find out how selfish they are, six months after they've gotten married? Why do lazy, minimum-effort employees always seem to find work in places where they feel underappreciated? This new group of people you've been hanging out with—why are they starting to treat you and say the same things about you as the old group of people did? Why are you beginning to feel as peeved and upset toward them as toward everybody else who's thought those things?

Because maybe not all the problem is your spouse. Maybe not all the problem is your employer. Maybe not everybody is conspiring together to come to the same conclusion about you.

Maybe it's just . . . the truth.

And the truth is what God is always wanting you to see. Because when you're dealing with the truth, that's when you can actively work toward real change.

So maybe it's time for you to pull out the shovel and hand tools, as opposed to the easy push of the lawn mower. Time for sanctification to become a personal process for yourself, not just a personal assignment for somebody else.

If you expect things to change, you can't just keep mowing over the stuff that keeps cropping up, every time the people with whom you rub shoulders start rubbing you the wrong way. If the heart of the problem is the problem of the heart—which it is— you'll never cure the disease you're suffering from by doing X-rays on other people.

Addictions

We realize, of course, the complex web of mental, emotional, and physical components that mix together to create addictive behaviors. Many, many people suffering from drug, alcohol, and other addictions have found their way to our church by God's sweet providence, and have found freedom from their enslavements through His gospel and His sanctifying grace. But not without struggle. Not without serious measures being taken. So don't think we're relegating addiction recovery to these next couple of point-and-click paragraphs. We're just making one general observation that has proven true over and over again.

The emergency triage setup that most people run screaming toward, at the height of their addictions, is whatever will help them make the behavior stop. They just want to quit. They don't want to do this anymore. And that's certainly a wise, positive first step in the right direction. But if any of us who battle addictions treat only the surface issues—the presenting symptoms—without working to figure out what's actually spawning the pain from deep down inside, we're dooming ourselves to what the prophet

Jeremiah called "'peace, peace,' when there is no peace" (Jer. 6:14). White-knuckled abstinence where there is no healing.

Because without going down into your heart to see what's truly wrong—even if you sort of succeed at stopping the drinking or abusing or whatever—you'll just trade out one addiction for another. You'll swap the one you hate for another one you can tolerate. But it'll just be a new weed growing from the same root. And you still won't be free, even if you're sober.

That's what comes from "mowing over." And the deception of it all is that it usually feels right. We want our addiction to stop; so we try to make it stop. We want a relationship with less drama; we go out and find one with less drama. Feels good. Feels better. For now.

But God wants more for us than "feels good for now." He wants us free forever. He's already done everything required to *position* us with eternal amounts of holiness and identity. We've been fully justified and adopted. So why would a God who would do all that, at the sacrificial cost of His own Son, want to see us chained to a revolving door of unhealthy relationships and substitute addictions in the meantime? Doesn't it make sense that His desire is to see us at liberty to *manifest* the blessings of gospel freedom from now into next year, the next ten years, the next fifty years? To see us growing and changing, renewing, transforming? Being steadily sanctified?

That's why He's not willing to let us stop at just mowing things over. He wants that yard of ours to be thick and lush, not all clover and dandelions, not the stuff that burns up and turns brown in the heat of mid-July, gouging your feet every time you walk to the mailbox.

No, mowing over sin just won't cut it.

And neither will this option: *covering it up.*

"Covering up" is a second barrier that threatens to hinder the progress of our sanctification. It's the "How you doing; I'm fine" approach to handling just about everything that comes at us in life, from the most casual conversation even to the most personal relationship.

And it's easier to pull off today than ever. Social media—as if we needed another way of masking ourselves behind these heavily edited, skin-lotioned personas of ours—has basically tossed us the keys to the family car. Now we can show everybody in the world (from our next-door neighbors to our old high school friends) what lovely dates we go on with our spouse, what smiley vacations we take with the kids. Pop on a Bible verse, upload a cool picture, write a touching blog post, and we're the envied image of all our friends.

If only it were so true . . .

But isn't the whole idea of sanctification the fact that we're not really there yet? That we're still growing and becoming? Still learning how to live the gospel out? Then why this obsession with pretending to be something for other people, who are pretending to be something for us? It's madness. You see that, don't you?

The cross of Jesus, while definitely meant to *include* us in the family of God, is also designed to *out* us as people who desperately need what its forgiveness and power provide. The redeeming work of Christ, therefore, is not a means of making us superhuman. It actually reveals us as being *very* human, as men and women who depend totally and only on God. We don't bring Him glory by being so amazingly strong; we bring Him glory, the Bible says, by boasting "gladly" of our weaknesses "so that the power of Christ may rest upon [us]" (2 Cor. 12:9).

And one of the most beautiful ways His power and presence operates in us—sanctifying us—is through the living, breathing friendship of those brothers and sisters who know *exactly* who we are, what we struggle with, where we've failed, and how we sometimes still tremble before our old fears and bad habits.

The two of us can attest to this. When the fellow believers in our lives are calling us up to check on us, to ask us probing questions, to see how we've been applying the promises of God to our most troubling sin areas, we don't feel busted and intruded upon, like, "How dare you insinuate such a thing!" No, it's a regular, encouraging reminder from God, spoken through the caring voice of our friends, that He is fighting our battles for us on all fronts, that He's right here with us, doing whatever it takes to grant us the ability to be obedient.

But you can never experience that feeling if you just slip in and out the back door at church and never let anybody get to know you. You can never tap into that kind of strength if your default is to act like you're too good for it.

Covering up is just dumb. You're not gaining a thing by doing it, except keeping yourself enslaved to your secrets. And if you're being honest with yourself, you know this is true. Do you struggle with sexual immorality? Then confess it. With anger? Confess it. With lust? Just go ahead and confess it. With embarrassing addictions? Yes. Get it out there. The best way to start stripping it of its power is to drag that dark monster into the light. How could that be any worse than what it's already done and is still doing to you?

Sanctification will always be a process. And we've each got enough disease and dysfunction to fill a whole lifetime of learning sessions. But we can crank the setting to warp speed—and actually start enjoying the right-now blessings and benefits of an unhypocritical, "undivided mind" (Ps. 86:11 HCSB)—by becoming militant in a couple of key areas: not lightly *mowing over* our sins, and not keeping them *covered up*, out of public view.

Imagine what could change from those two changes.

Power Steering

Every time you pull out of the driveway from the house you've recently moved into, there's a new way for you to go places from the way you went before, from your old house. A new way to get to the interstate, a new way to get to your job, a new way to get the ball park, a new way to get to the hair salon. Everything's a little different now, requiring different kinds of turns, learning a new arrangement of streets and intersections and how they all connect together.

But the more you learn about life in this new neighborhood, and the more familiar you become with the landmarks and the map grid, the less likely you'll become to get lost and turned around. You'll know where you are, you'll know where to go, and you'll know how to get there.

"Therefore, brothers, since we have confidence"—confidence in the "new and living way" that's been opened up for us through the blood of Christ—let us "draw near" and "hold fast" to the promises of our Faithful One and the confession of our belief in Him. And knowing the right way to go, let us not only summon up the courage to follow this new path for ourselves, but also commit to help "stir up" one another, as each of us follows the sanctified paths that can take us safely in and out, and always back home (Heb. 10:19–25).

Right turns only. As we look to Him, He can do it.

Together, we can do it.

Chapter 7

The Perfect Storm

Guilt, Shame, and Aftershocks

In late October 2012, only days before Halloween, a Category 2 hurricane churning north from the Caribbean collided under a full moon with a ferocious winter storm that had been howling across the upper Midwest. Adding to the high-energy mix was a chilling blast of arctic air descending rapidly out of Canada—the classic Nor'easter—dropping temperatures well below freezing in advance of the approaching precipitation.

The National Weather Service had warned of a "hybrid vortex" being created by the confluence of these massive footprints. Observers were monitoring extremely low pressure in the central Atlantic, which was pushing the hurricane toward land after remaining just off the coast for a number of days, building strength over open waters. By the time it rammed the beaches along the Jersey Shore and Long Island on October 29, packing sustained winds of 80 mph, the harrowing effects of these combined weather elements could be felt as far inland as Ohio and Kentucky—a nasty double whammy of raging waves at sea, as well as white-out blizzard conditions across the mountainous interior.

It was dubbed "Frankenstorm."

More officially, Superstorm Sandy.

Altogether, it killed 125 people in the United States, inflicting more than $60 billion in damage, leveling numerous homes and businesses, pouring floodwater into tunnels and subway stations, and causing widespread power outages and gasoline shortages across much of the eastern third of the country.

Unprecedented calamity.

And yet as historic as Sandy proved to be in the meteorological history of America, many people today experience internally a similar, tag-team convergence of storms, almost in a never-ending loop. The thunder that can all too steadily echo in our hearts from the tandem interaction of *guilt* and *shame* is often enough to keep us awake at night, if not torturing us throughout the day with its persistent pounding.

We know that life wasn't meant to be like this.

And we know it won't be this way forever.

But for now, everywhere the sweep of that guilt-and-shame radar circulates, it's almost sure to detect another incoming threat, whether a passing shower, an overnight downpour, or those one-after-another bands of severe storm systems, firing up new tornado watches and warnings in their wake.

And yet part of the promise of this gospel song—as we sing it throughout the dark hallways of conscience and condemnation—is to lessen not only their one-two punch, but to rob them of the power to do any more collateral damage.

Come on in. You'll see what we mean.

Inside Jobbed

Having done a flyover of some key gospel ideas throughout the first half of this book, we're now beginning our descent pattern, bringing this payload of biblical truth down to the ground, where the Spirit of God can taxi its arrival into your everyday life. And even if the view from 30,000 feet left you feeling a little dizzy, we don't think there's any chance you're going to miss making connections between the stuff we're about to cover and the experiences that occupy your routine travel schedule.

First stop is very familiar territory: guilt and shame.

These two scourges on the human heart made an early visit to our planet, emerging amid the disintegration of innocence and honor that happened in the Garden of Eden. And throughout all these years, they've never seen fit to leave. So while a lot of us could probably attest that we saw one or both of them on the street today or in a back bedroom as recently as this morning, the nature of guilt and shame—as with all of the Serpent's weapons—pegs them as being very tricky and deceptive. Even in knowing them by first name, there's a lot we often *don't* know about them, a lot they don't just come right out and reveal about themselves.

For instance, we're often accustomed to seeing guilt and shame together, as if they're twins, a matching set, virtually synonymous with one another. And even though they do tend to overlap and interact with each other, they're really not quite the same thing. While both of them do indicate the falling short of some kind of standard, the one that *guilt* fails to meet is more often a clear moral code, a legality. The standard that *shame* fails to meet, on the other hand, goes much deeper to the core of who we really are. Our identity.

Let's say, for example, that you view yourself as a caring, giving person, sacrificial, unselfish, always willing to help people in need. So when you pass by a homeless man on the street, or when they advertise another ministry opportunity at church, you may experience feelings of *guilt* if you don't do something, as if you're breaking a rule or law. But because this do-everything aspect of your nature is a sizable part of your self-image—a place where you derive a lot of your worth, value, and identity—something deeper is going on as well. You feel *shame* for not truly being the person you claim or want to be.

See the subtle difference? Same could go for just about any element that comprises the phantom "you" that you envision in your head—your desired image, what you want people to think of you, what you wish so badly to be true about yourself. When that person doesn't show up in real life, when the real you is a lot uglier, meaner, embarrassing, or unlikeable than this, that's when you're likely to feel ashamed of yourself.

Guilt is more about what we *do*; shame is more about who we *are*. It's important to see this distinction.

The parts we usually try changing first—the anger, the abuse, the lust (each of which we'll be addressing in this chapter)—only represent the fruit that's growing on the end of the stem. Pick it off, and you haven't really killed it, because a new one will immediately start growing where the old one used to be. But if you'll get down underneath this thing, take an axe to the base of the trunk, there shouldn't be a whole lot of branch left anymore for that rotten fruit to start budding on again.

And what you'll often find down there in the roots, when you go to digging, are both a hunger for innocence and a hunger for honor. *Guilt* (robbing us of innocence) and *shame* (robbing us of honor) are the double helix that creates the DNA of our worst behavior.

Guilt

Guilt is a little bit easier than shame to recognize and isolate. We often stand a pretty good chance of connecting the dots between the pain we're feeling and the thing we did (or didn't do), which then gives us a much cleaner shot at repenting of it. Of changing it.

But we do possess some convoluted ways of either blurring its source or confusing our conscience. That's why we can sometimes *feel* guilty and not actually *be* guilty of anything (false guilt), or we can sometimes *be* guilty of something and not really *feel* any guilt from it (hardheartedness)—even to the point of glorying in our wrongdoing, celebrating our independence and lawlessness as almost a badge of honor. It's completely backward. And yet it can lead to so many other issues in our lives.

True guilt is not really a feeling at all; it's a state of being. If we do something we shouldn't, if we participate in something we know we don't have any business being around, then we're guilty. Plain and simple. And obviously, something needs to be done about that.

But we need to recognize when the standard we've apparently violated—the one that's causing us to feel a measure of guilt as a result—is perhaps not *God's* standard. Not the *Bible's* standard. For instance, if you're a person who's wired to feel guilty unless you're constantly busy and doing things, never able to slow down and experience Sabbath rest with a clear conscience, then *you're* the one setting the standard that you're breaking. Or if your husband comes home complaining about how dirty and disorganized the house is, after you've been wrangling kids and picking bubble gum out of somebody's hair all day, then *he's* the one setting the standard that makes you feel like a bad wife.

But guilt can explode off of any of these launchpads—from actual disobedience, as well as from yourself and from others. And when it does, it often leads to the kinds of behaviors and angry reactions that start leading you more in the direction of . . .

Shame

Shame, in contrast with guilt, can sort of float around in the iced tea glass. You see it, you know it's there, you dig your spoon down to fish it out, but it proves a lot more elusive and hard to pull up than you expect.

We can feel shame for all sorts of random things. Some people feel shame because they don't have much money. Some people feel shame about the car they drive or the house where they live. Some people feel shame about the family they come from, the school they went to, the size of their wedding ring, or the shape of their body. Some even feel ashamed—at least within certain circles—of being a Christian, or of doing what's right and morally courageous against the pressure of other people's more cosmopolitan opinions.

So shame can obviously coil and strike from a wide variety of ground cover. And even though it may not have a right to be on our property or to set up shop around the corner, shame is painful when it hits us from wherever it's coming from.

But what's hard to see at times like these is that there's nothing shameful about being poor or making a modest income. There's nothing shameful about driving a car that still requires you to turn and look out the back windshield when you're pulling away from a parking place. There's nothing shameful about not living in a neighborhood where the residents pay $1,000 every other month to keep everybody's grass the same length. That's illegitimate shame. Nor have you done anything shameful yourself just because someone has taken advantage of your innocence and vulnerability as a sick way of meeting their own distorted needs. But if you sense and process shame that's originating from these and other similar sources, it can still succeed at making you feel worthless, unloved, dirty, less-than . . . even if you've done nothing at all to warrant it. It can make you want to cope with it by covering and hiding.

That's not guilt; that's shame.

And the question it begs . . . is why?

Why are we so ashamed of ourselves, of these things?

The answer, really, is pretty simple. Shame is deeply rooted in identity. And the "self-ideal" we create for ourselves can often incorporate a lot of expectations that simply aren't included in *God's* ideal for us. We can exalt the wrong kind of perfect. We can select the wrong kind of heroes. We can decide that the touched-up look of magazine covers, the perks of a certain tax bracket, the personality of our old college roommate, and the postings on people's Facebook pages represent the life we should be living and the image we should be projecting. But where's that pressure coming from? What are those wants being driven by?

And how much of your violent temper, your binge drinking, your sexual promiscuity, your most troubling addictions—the physical symptoms of *anger*, *abuse*, and *lust*—arise not just from a generically bad heart, but are actually being fueled by shame? And guilt? Or maybe both—in an ongoing, killer storm?

Pop-up Storms

Guilt and shame don't just exist out there by themselves on the weather map, like a stationary front that remains in its own little jet stream. No, they will almost always affect the rest of the forecast for your life—the ranges of temperature and other prevailing conditions. They will stir up sinful thoughts within you, will tell you how you're supposed to feel, will cause chaos to spiral around you, and will make you want to do just about anything to stop the sting of that clawing sensation—especially from shame, which is perhaps the most painful emotion known to man. Then they'll begin turning into steady behavioral patterns—the things you do that you just absolutely hate about yourself.

Guilt and shame are underneath nearly all of it.

So see if the following progression has rung true in your own life, because we've certainly seen it in our own. We're not quoting textbooks here. We get it. We identify.

It usually starts with the surfacing of *anger*—something more along the lines of self-hate at first. We're kicking ourselves. We want to punish ourselves. We're so mad at how STUPID we can be sometimes. How many years has it been now? And still not seeming to get any better at this. No stronger. No smarter. We thought we'd be so much further along by now. But we're as lame and lousy as ever. Weak and predictable. Just like everybody thinks. Just like everybody says. Just like everybody would see . . . if they really knew us, if they knew what we were like.

Let that frustration of guilt and shame keep building, and one heart becomes unable to hold it all in. From here we tend to gravitate in a couple of different directions—or both—trying to manage these runaway feelings, this lowered sense of personal worth and value. First, we feel as though other people are justified in seeing us as rather worthless too. So we begin treating ourselves cheaply, not taking care of our bodies and our diet, being casual with our haunts and our habits, making it easier to be taken advantage of and looked down on. But secondly (or simultaneously), the same insecurities can also express themselves as anger turned outward. In rages and short fuses. We attack and tear down, control and manipulate. If *we* can't be happy, then no one else deserves to be happy. If *we* can't feel good about ourselves, we'll make sure we're giving others some mighty good reasons why they don't have any right to feel so good about themselves either.

Anger has now turned into *abuse*—abuse of others, abuse of ourselves. We carelessly enter into unhealthy situations and relationships where sin is only a wink of approval away. We turn against even the people who are closest to us, abusing them with our quick-tempered mouths, our physical aggression, our emotional dirty tricks and blackmail.

And then from bad to worse, because abuse also has a nasty way of coupling together with *lust* and sexual immorality, diminishing not only the dignity that God has created into us as human beings, but reducing other people into the dehumanized objects of our own pleasure, as if they don't have a soul, or a life, or any other purpose in that fleeting moment besides satisfying our lustful craving.

One of the main reasons why people go off the rails into sexual flirtation, affairs, and pornography is because guilt and shame have so cheapened what they see of themselves, they lose the ability to see the true value in anyone else—people who've been fashioned by God with intrinsic worth, not to give pleasure to *us*, but to find pleasure in *Him*.

God's glorious, creative design for sex is meant to point toward the oneness of His sacred covenant with us, as pictured in the covenant oneness of marriage. So within that exclusive relationship, it is ultimately an act of worship—worship of His grace and goodness, extended to us through the gospel—as opposed to how Satan distorts the sexual act into sexual immorality, into worship of another kind: worship of safety, feelings, security, people, acceptance, worshiping the "creature" rather than the "Creator" (Rom. 1:25).

Women who would never dream of selling their bodies for money, like a common prostitute, sell it for something else instead: for the "feeling" of love, for relationship, being made for even an hour to feel wanted, desirable, and beautiful. Men seek to squelch their own insecurities by fantasizing about other women, collecting trophies for themselves on the wallpaper of their minds, seeking redemption for the shame they carry around inside, but finding it always to be a counterfeit redemption.

And the storms just keep coming. Pouring down. Bouncing off each other and setting off new ones. Guilt and shame continue to spark our anger, fuel our abuse, feed our lust. And if all we do to try putting out the flames is to airdrop sin repellent from above, hoping to stamp them out around the edges, there will always be more than enough oxygen available to keep them burning on into the night.

Surely the gospel has a way to stop this craziness.

Storm Chasers

Jesus' disciples, when they saw the sky darkening with storm clouds, probably thought they had nothing to worry about. After all, most of them knew their way around the water. They'd learned from long experience how to handle even the most unexpected things that could come up at sea—not without running it close sometimes, maybe—but at least they'd always been able to make it back to shore. Nothing had killed them yet.

Besides, Jesus was in the boat this time. In fact, He was the one who'd told them to pitch out and sail over to the other side. But there must have been something about this particular storm, the longer it raged and the more violently it tossed their little vessel, that outdid the ones they'd battled before. And Jesus or no Jesus, they didn't know what to do. "Master, Master, we are perishing!" they cried, shaking Him wide awake from a sound sleep.

He eased up from His resting berth, patiently climbed top-side, stood facing into the teeth of the storm, told the wind and the waves they had no authority to sink this boat . . . and suddenly, everything stilled into a breathtaking, speechless calm.

The disciples stood there in awe, looking from one face to another, asking through silent eyes if everyone else was seeing the same thing *they* were seeing. Then Jesus interrupted their dazed wonderment with a simple question which cut through the emotions of the moment and brought the whole thing into ultimate focus:

"Where is your faith?" (Luke 8:25).

Jesus always asks the perfect question. And as we begin to sort through and clean up from the wreckage left behind by our own powerful storms of guilt and shame, His question—"Where is your faith?"—remains the one that leads us to our best answers. So, to borrow from what we discussed in the previous chapter, it's high time to *vivify*—to dive right into the deeps of biblical truth, rediscovering what God has done through the gospel to dispel these dark, angry clouds so we can sail with Him calmly into safe harbor. And with much less baggage.

Justification

We're going back a couple of chapters now, picking up the element of the gospel that forms the antidote for the banging windows and shutters of guilt. It's the banging gavel of your Judge, declaring you pardoned and given innocence by the blood of Jesus Christ.

"You, who were dead in your trespasses and the uncircumcision of your flesh," the Bible says, "God made alive together with him, having forgiven us *all* our trespasses—"

Wait, let's stop here for a second. "All" is a very basic word. Three letters. Really only two, since a pair of them show up back-to-back. Can't get much easier to spell and pronounce, nor much harder to misunderstand. Our God has forgiven us "*all* our trespasses, by canceling the record of debt that stood against us with its legal demands. This he set aside, nailing it to the cross" (Col. 2:13–14).

So—

That sense of condemnation you feel for things you've done in the past that you've tried as hard as you can to confess and repent of . . .

That struggle you're having right now with a sinful, frustrating habit or tendency that's become such a natural part of the way you react to stress and insecurity . . .

Those doubts you carry around, not sure you'll *ever* be able to overcome the squeezing grip of this particular sin in your life, no matter how long you keep trying . . .

Let's just say there's a gospel app for that. For *all* of that. The cancelling of your debt by the forgiving blood of the Lamb means the guilt from all your sin is gone—past, present, and future—as well as all your reasons for allowing guilt to crank itself up into angry fits and other defensive measures. You've been pardoned. You're free. You've been given innocence.

Believe it. And be changed by it.

But because we do still sin, and because we continue needing a way to counteract these shortcomings, there's also . . .

Sanctification

People looking for loopholes in the gospel—as we humans have been doing all the way back into the first century—like to wave this banner of justification as an excuse for lightening up on their practice of holiness. Having been declared forgiven, they guess it means free time in the clubs, and no guilt for a cover charge. It's sort of the same way a certain stripe of Christian mechanics or plumbers or real estate pros may be inclined to think they can lean on that fish symbol in the corner of their business card, not really needing to put out their best work all the time, since people will always be inclined to be more forgiving and understanding of them. After all, we're Christians here, aren't we?

But just as the true joy of working is found not in lazing through long lunches and cutting corners the rest of the day, but rather through diligence and excellence and full service of others' needs, our lives as believers grow richer and more satisfying as we bring our daily best to the altar, experiencing even deeper closeness with the Father.

What you're feeling, even as a Christian, when you cross the lines and boundaries that your good and loving God has put into place for your protection, is true guilt. It's really there. But by the undying nature of His covenant love, He continues to patiently work with us through our weakness and fallenness, urging godly repentance from our hearts, and thereby short-circuiting the other sinful spinoffs that can piggyback onto the guilt of our repeated failures.

Jesus' question is relevant here: "Where is your faith?" Rather than endlessly staring at our shortcomings or continuing on hopelessly in our sin, we can return to Him and find again our desires for innocence.

Adoption

Finally, as we mentioned earlier in the chapter, the Genesis 1 and 2 ideal was marked, among other things, by *innocence* and *honor*. Human beings were created to stand taller than all the other species that populated the planet. And more than just living in a perfectly guilt-free paradise, the Bible says "the man and his wife were both naked and not ashamed" (Gen. 2:25). Imagine that. Think about what daily life is often like for you—the moods and feelings inside your own head and heart. How cool would it be to live in a relationship without even a darting shadow of shame, where you could be completely yourself without any fear of rejection, without any fear of abusing or being abused. Must've died and gone to heaven.

Or must've been adopted by your heavenly Father.

Nothing drives away shame any faster than the thought of being fully known and yet still loved, enjoyed, and delighted in by the one who knows you the best. No longer is shame a valid analysis of a Christian's past, his property value, her marriage prospects, or their educational prowess and buying power. God loves us and has adopted us exactly as we are, knowing every single thing about us. And if *He's* not ashamed of us, then why should *we* be?

Therefore, shame begins to vanish when we realize we can be utterly open and confessional before our God as well as before others, especially our family of faith. The best way to make sure that shame cannot grow in our hearts—and cannot by nature continue to grow into anger, abuse, and lust—is simply by not keeping any more secrets.

And why *should* you? Because the truth is, there *are* no secrets. Even if nobody but God knows certain secrets about you, the weight of those secrets is the root beneath almost all your depression, your disgust with yourself, your coolness toward worship, your obsession with keeping yourself covered and mysterious, hard to pin down. Hard to be known.

Secrets only lead to more shame.

But look at the father in the story we call the Parable of the Prodigal Son. In reality, this tale that Jesus told is not so much about the runaway barhopping boy, or even his sour, self-righteous brother back home, but rather the father who entreats *both* of them to come in and experience the full bounty of relationship with him. It's about a dad's absolute delight in his stubborn, foolish children who each have found their own pathway into shame, and yet can never be unloved by the one who calls them his own.

Here at The Village, when we conduct baptism services, we invite new converts to stand in the water and lay out the reasons for the shame they once bore. They tell of where God found them, what they were like, who they represented themselves to be, how they characterized their identity for all those years of their lives. You'd think the prospect of being asked to share this stuff might keep the numbers down, might cause people to shy away from the humiliation. How many men and women have the guts to say it, to admit to it—right out there in front of God and everybody?

Only one answer works: Through the adoptive nature of the gospel, they've realized they are fully known by a Father who fully delights in them. They're not *bragging* about their shame; they're bragging about a God who is greater than their shame. They're not minimizing sin; they're glorying in the sufficiency of Christ.

Think of how the prodigal most likely felt, once he realized his father was welcoming him home as a son instead of laying into him with a sermon. Relief. Wow. Didn't really expect that. *Great, well . . . wonderful. Think I'll just go up and take a shower, get into some clean clothes.* But, no. His dad was throwing a party—the kind (the Bible says) you could hear out in the street. The throbbing bass, the loud singing, the peals of laughter. You can almost imagine the prodigal trying to talk his father out of it. "No, no, let's not do all that." He didn't really want *everybody* to know where he'd been, what he'd done.

Yeah, it's strangely rather difficult for us to be loved so well, accepted and adored so fully, to be delighted in by our Father, by anybody. Because, hey, we don't even delight in ourselves, in who we are. How in the world could God—the One who knows it *all* (there's that word again)—find a whole lot of anything to be crazy about in us?

But that's what slings the storm of shame back to the wicked west where it came from, and plants in our yard a strong, new tree of honor and identity that can withstand the next roar of foul weather brewing hot out there on the horizon. It's what keeps us grounded and secure, without all the anger, abuse, and lust that were once the only things we thought could hold us together, our only safe-place solutions from how shame made us feel.

The gospel gives it all.

Justification for our guilt.

Sanctification for deconstructing our false ideals.

Adoption for the red face of our secret shame.

And suddenly, in place of the raw emotions that continually joined forces against us, knocking us around like a nickel in a clothes dryer, the sun can now rise in the morning on a *truly* perfect storm, as God's grace feeds in us a new passion for Him, and passion responds by feeding us even more grace—a revitalizing shower where the only water seeping into our hearts is from the fountain of living waters, replenishing our once-guilty, once-shameful hearts with sheer joy, acceptance, and freedom.

Let it rain.

Chapter 8

God Is Great, God Is Good

Fighting Fear and Anxiety

Okay, this is just Matt talking here for a few minutes. We felt like the best way to begin this chapter, which addresses a second pair of underlying threats (in addition to guilt and shame), would be by letting me speak directly to you from my heart, from an up close and personal perspective.

You may or may not know that several years ago, I experienced a fairly violent seizure at home one morning—completely out of the blue—triggered by what turned out to be a mass that had begun developing in my right frontal lobe. Brain cancer. Deadly serious.

As a result, I underwent what's called a craniotomy—which, for me, basically required cutting a big chunk out of my brain. That's how invasive the problem was. And after making it through that lovely ordeal, I was then sentenced to eighteen months of chemo, six weeks of radiation, and a warning from medical experts that for the rest of my life, I must frequently be rescanned and reevaluated, making sure the cancer doesn't come back. They tell me it will.

Of course, they also told me I should be dead by now.

They obviously don't know *everything*.

But in case you've never been through anything that's on a scale of this life-threatening magnitude, here's a little taste of what that white-coat encounter can be like. When doctors say, "Matt, you probably have two or three years to live," based on the prognosis for a cancer of this kind, they're not talking about three exhilarating, blowout years of skydiving and world travel and checking new items off your bucket list. What they foresee in your future are two or three years where, in hopes of saving you, they will poison you and torture you and render you miserably fatigued and uncomfortable for weeks at a time, after which (they anticipate) you'll likely grow nearly nonexistent toward the end, before dying of the whole thing anyway.

How nice.

Definitely not a Hallmark movie.

So, as you can imagine, when the subject of fear and anxiety comes up—having been on the receiving end of that kind of conversation—I've got a pretty good handle on what I'm talking about. I know exactly how it feels to lie in bed at night, stare up into the suffocating darkness, and worry myself sick about my kids, about my wife, about myself . . . about everything. I know how quickly my body can tense up whenever I feel a certain pain or a wave of uneasiness, how my mind can jerk the steering wheel hard to the right and then need a few minutes to collect itself by the side of the road. Like you perhaps, I don't have to look very far to pinpoint some real reasons for concern. Some of my worst nightmares, in fact, include actual film footage that weaves itself into and out of the drama.

Nobody wants this, I guarantee you.

Thankfully, though, God in His grace gave me a period of years in which nearly all the other fellow patients I'd come to know, people who'd been diagnosed with primary brain cancer around the same time as I'd been treated, seemed to be doing great. Including me. Battling well. Which was really encouraging. To all of us. But then, in what was almost a rash of back-to-back events, two or three of them died within weeks and months of each other. And upon hearing the news—or in some cases, after having personally conducted their funerals—a chilly groan of anxious thoughts and worries would come echoing down the hallway at me, settling down with a thud in my gut.

Would I be next?

Is this really going to get me?

Am I doing everything I can do?

Scary.

But even in the midst of a genuine crisis like mine and my family's—or in the midst of a similar scene of adversity in your own life—or even in the midst of fears and anxieties that don't yet possess a name or a face, or a medical term, or a probable duration, or anything other than the shoe-dropping panic of what might be (and what you're already scared to death of) . . .

The gospel of Jesus Christ is still the one reassuring answer to your antsy heart.

And actually, to a whole lot more.

Peace of the Puzzle

The Garden of Eden, as we've seen, reveals to us the ideal for which God created mankind—the state of perfect relationship that continues to stir a jealous longing inside of us, drawing us toward the only One who can remake what's been broken and left for dead.

Within this paradise, of course, we've identified the presence of innocence and honor, each of which burned to a crisp on the scorched earth of original sin, being transformed into the bitter realities of guilt and shame. But also present at the beginning of time, before the introduction of sin and loss, were qualities that represented the functional opposites of our current fears and anxieties.

Eden was, by contrast, a place of *peace* and *prosperity*.

Adam, for example, was never going to fall out of a tree and break his neck. He and Eve would never feel the need to sleep in separate parts of the garden, waiting for one or the other's temper to cool down, or perhaps going to see if anybody else was possibly out there who might make a good divorce lawyer. Their daily work was hard but never laborious—always plentiful, always reward-ing—as enjoyable and pleasurable as anything else they'd be doing later on that evening. They never experienced lack or shortage, worry or doubt, suspicions or night sweats—anything that sig-naled a deficiency of trust or personal contentment.

But when the announcement came down, declaring that death had now entered their existence—

Let's just say we don't have a comparison emotion to match what these two must've felt. When we're told today that we're going to die, in a world where every morning's newspaper contains a full two pages or more of obituary notices, we're at least familiar with the concept, even if we're not exactly crazy about our name being attached to it. But having never even known a single, solitary feeling of sadness or shock, much less the idea that they might not be able to catch a breath one day, that their bodies would be forced to return to the dust where they came from . . .

That was fear of another color.

Seemed impossible. Unheard of.

And so, beginning from that tragic point in time, fear and anxiety began aggravating the human heart, so that even His redeemed children through the ages, down to this very day, would know the cruel feeling of being robbed, of living without the peace and prosperity He'd intended for us to enjoy.

But that's not all we need to know before being able to dig into these specific fears of ours. That's not all we need to know before allowing God to turn them into something that calms and encourages us instead. The peace and prosperity that existed in the lives of Adam and Eve before the Fall were not goals they had sought for themselves and had somehow been able to attain. Ease and abundance were not their endgame—a calculated pursuit of desired circumstances and living conditions. No, the source of their confident certainty was simply God alone. God Himself. As long as they were in fellowship with Him, they could forever expect His blessings to just roll downhill and right into their lives. *He* was their righteousness, *He* was their innocence, *He* was their sense of identity, *He* was their dignity and honor.

He was their peace.

And *He* was their prosperity.

He was the reason they felt no fear.

So even though we're confined today to a much different time zone than the one Adam and Eve set their clocks to—back before the Fall struck thirteen and threw everything out of whack—the winning response to fear and anxiety remains completely one-dimensional.

It's Him—not the favorable resolution of our problems.

It's Him—not the removal of every worst-case scenario.

It's Him—not an easy, breezy, adversity-free lifestyle.

It's Him. It has always been and will always be Him.

That's why He chose to introduce Himself to us in Scripture as the "God of all comfort" (2 Cor. 1:3), who is able in all our suffering to give us something far superior to any other source of relief. More than an encouraging doctor's report. More than a positive parent-teacher conference. More than the manufacturer's guaranteed bumper-to-bumper warranty. While these good-news moments and insurance policies can set our minds at ease for a little while—at least till the next challenge comes along—God desires instead to give us His own self as our eternal "Abba" Father (Rom. 8:15), our ever-present help and all-sufficient provider, our sole reason for not being so afraid.

Abba. It's a term that doesn't actually mean "Daddy," the way a lot of people will tell you. (Jews living in that historical time and place would've never dreamed of using such a casual means of parental address. It would've been the height of disrespect.) For while "Abba" does connote a level of family intimacy, it sends up more of the idea that "my dad can beat up your dad," that our Father is not caught off guard or pushed around by anything that seems too big or oversized for us, no matter *what* it is.

And that's why life is still allowed to be tough on us. To be fearful and frightening. Even on His kids. Because instead of giving us a pass-code escape from every potential headache or heartache, instead of steering us around every minefield that lies between our current coordinates and the places His love will take us, God's desire is to walk us straight through our fears to the other side . . . in order to show us that we didn't really have anything to be so afraid of in the first place.

Not as long as *He's* here.

Not with the Prince of Peace in charge.

Believe it or not, fears and anxieties do not get the last, worrisome word when it comes to how we face the pressures and problems of life. But that doesn't mean God can't turn their fevered voice into something utterly redemptive for us. For when we look through His wisdom and power at those things that possess the strongest ability to scare and alarm us—the things that leave us feeling the most nervous and fidgety—we can begin to wrap the warm blanket of the gospel around those specific issues, the places in our heart that still ache for what He's actually already done. We can begin to do something better with fear than just sit around being afraid of it.

We can start to see a change.

A Sacred Trust

Fear, like anger, is not always a bad thing. Healthy fear is what makes us jump out of the way of a moving truck—or more generally, it's what makes us keep to the sidewalk instead of ever stepping out into the traffic to begin with. People who do not own this kind of fear are either psychotic or are brandishing a bulletproof sense of invincibility, which will surely succeed at killing them one day if they continue to live like they're fifteen.

So there is definitely such a thing as legitimate fear. Reasoned fear. Things to be properly disliked and avoided.

But there are also many *illegitimate* fears, worries that contain no real substance or basis for belief except in the fretful reaches of our wild imaginations. We're talking about the debilitating "what-ifs" of life, the kind that strip us of all joy and stability, the kind that can paralyze us even in the middle of a good, bright, sunshiny day—so insidiously that we can't even enjoy what's happening directly in front of us for fear of what might be coming around the corner.

Yet every one of these fears—both the real and the imagined—give us some instructive information about ourselves. *They tell us what we value most in life.* They tell us where we've centered the bulk of our attention. Better than any of our well-spoken arguments and justifications could ever accomplish, they tell us the exact placement of our priorities. Because the greater amount of worth we ascribe to certain things, then the more fear and anxiety will naturally orbit around those very points.

Again, we're not defining these broad subjects as being either good or bad. That's not the objective here. Most of us, for example, are fairly inclined to worry a good deal in regard to our children, to be concerned about their health and their friendships, their feelings and their futures. Sometimes our fears and anxieties over them can become almost the entire topic of thought and conversation for full weekends at a time. Why, do you think, would their issues rise to such a level of primary importance in our eyes? Because we value our kids so highly.

But everything that exists around us on earth—from appliances and possessions, to people and relationships, even to the children who live right here under our roof—any of them are capable of becoming an idol that drains away our trust in the sufficiency and sovereignty of God. As a result, we're left feeling the futile need to reestablish control over what (in our judgment) He is obviously not handling in a manner that's acceptable to us or feels safe to us.

If we begin to drift spiritually in that direction, seeking to take over His job as best we can, our fears will become more and more unhealthy, more self-centered, more rooted in pride and presumption. And we'll slide further away all the time from the trusting, contented place where His gospel invites our hearts to rest.

"Light momentary affliction" is how the Bible describes the various adversities we endure in life—not that they're artificial or insignificant, not that God doesn't recognize how heavily they can press down on us. They're here. They're real. And they continue to circle back on us. Yet they do indeed pale in comparison with the "eternal weight of glory" He is preparing for us as His heirs, as His well-loved children (2 Cor. 4:17).

The truth is, every single thing that's troubling your mind right this minute—whether it's your health, your money, your car repairs, or your household heating system—your son's braces or your daughter's boyfriend, your credit score or your reputation, your sales quota or your insurance coverage, your remaining years of school, or the remaining inches around your waist—all of it will seem silly to you 20,000 years from now.

Know how we know? Because if you'd think back just *twenty* years, or *ten* years, or *five* years, or maybe even to *last* year, those concerns of yours that were strangling the life out of you during that particular snapshot of time would already—with few exceptions—appear "light" and "momentary" from the vantage point of where you're standing today. And when you reach your sixties or seventies or eighties (or whatever age is still future-tense for you— the way "forty" used to feel for us!), the fears that are screaming the loudest at you right now will almost certainly appear only modestly upsetting when seen solidly in your rear view.

Just think how they'll look from 20,000 years out.

We believe that's where Jesus was driving when He said, "Do not be anxious about your life, what you will eat or what you will drink, nor about your body, what you will put on. Is not life more than food, and the body more than clothing?" (Matt. 6:25). If you're familiar with this extended teaching from the Sermon on the Mount, you know how He went on to support His logic by pointing to the "birds of the air" (which are constantly supplied by God with their daily food) and the "lilies of the field" (which He decorates so beautifully despite their very short, seasonal life spans). But by the time Jesus wrapped up this lesson on anxiety, He had landed in basically the same place where we last saw Him out at sea in the previous chapter of this book, after quieting the storm that had spooked His disciples so badly. "Where is your faith?" He had asked them that day. "O you of little faith," He was saying to them now (v. 30). And to us.

Because it always comes back to faith.

It always comes down to the gospel.

The bottom line underneath most of our fear and anxiety is that we simply don't believe—don't have *faith*—in the goodness of God. To be a worrier means we don't trust He's going to provide for us, we don't think He's looking out for our best interests, we don't feel convinced that He's wise enough to know what to do for us, even if He does care and would do a better job of things if He could.

We doubt His *greatness*, and we doubt His *goodness*.

And until we come to the place where we're honest enough to admit this—to confess that the reason why we're so fearful is because we don't believe His rule over our lives is more compassionate and complete than our own personal OCD control is conditioned to be—then we'll never be able to move past it. Worry and dread will always have our number, and they'll mash on that 911 button every time we feel the slightest hiccup.

So ask yourself: Why *don't* you trust Him, after all He's done to save us from situations that are much more eternally impossible to untangle than any fears we could be facing today?

There are reasons why you don't. Understandable reasons, in fact. Perhaps your heart's been seriously misshapen by episodes of betrayal involving people from your past. Perhaps you've seen enough things go wrong in life, you're just built to be a little more cautious and skeptical, not willing to allow yourself to hope very easily. Perhaps you have a hard time not seeking to lay claim to more than your own share of responsibility, sort of that old "If you want it done right, do it yourself" kind of attitude. Just name it. Your analysis for why you're inclined toward distrust and dyspepsia could come from anywhere, from anything.

But today would be a good day to get this stuff out into the open, and to understand that whatever control you think you're exerting by being so careful and hesitant and micromanaging is really an elaborate illusion. And because of the gospel, a fruitless waste of time and energy.

You've been promised you will discover, once you determine to "seek first the kingdom of God and his righteousness," that He will make sure "all these things"—everything He knows you wisely need—"will be added to you" from a good Father's hand (Matt. 6:33). So there's no real need or purpose for collapsing into fear and worry. Not when you're covered *this* well. And the more you experience and apply this gospel-bought freedom—the more areas of your life that lose their ability to unnerve you—then the more you'll realize that He is increasingly becoming your primary love, the placeholder that so many other things in your life used to occupy, the One to whom you've ascribed your highest worth and value.

He is your peace.

Fear of the Dark

All right, it's Matt here again, to close it out.

My battle with cancer, as I mentioned, means that at regular intervals I'm expected to schedule follow-up brain scans to monitor my condition. I usually know about these procedures several months in advance—which gives me every day between now and then to know what's coming, and to imagine what horrors they might uncover this time when the doctors go to poking and prodding. Believe it or not, preachers are no more exempt from letting their thoughts go there than anybody else.

But as I sit here today, twisting the little reminder card in my fingers, the one that tells me I'll be back on that examination table sometime in January, I've got a choice to make. A gospel choice. Am I going to believe, as Jesus promised, that "today has enough trouble of its own" (Matt. 6:34 NIV), that I don't need to borrow any more from tomorrow, that He's already gone ahead of me into January, and therefore I'm able just to live out the balance of this one day—today—in full, twenty-four-hour celebration of His greatness and goodness? And when I wake up tomorrow before sunrise, even if the specter of January is the first thing there to greet me, am I not within my rights to tell it to move to one side, seeing as it's blocking my view of God's "new every morning" mercies (Lam. 3:22–23)?

I'm not saying for one minute that fears like mine—and fears like yours—are not founded in reality. Sometimes they actually are. This cancer could kill me. I know that. And there are moments when it scares the daylights out of me, days when I'd just as soon not be writing on the subject of anxiety but just wallowing around somewhere between self-pity and abject despair, completely giving in to the panic.

And so knowing this, I would say to you—if that portrayal comes close to describing how you often feel as well—quit pretending not to be scared. Be man or woman enough to say, "I'm afraid of this thing," even if your fear involves a matter of concern that others might think you crazy for even worrying about. The invitation of the gospel is to bring fear and anxiety out into the open, to "walk" them into "the light" (1 John 1:7). Because the way we deal with them is not by running from them, but by releasing them in broad daylight into the care and keeping of our

Father—by experiencing through a reconciled relationship with Him . . . *peace.*

When one of my friends passed away from cancer one weekend recently, I thought I was handling it pretty well. This woman loved the Lord, she was at peace with Him, and today she walks in glory with Him. Her faith has now become sight. I can praise God for that.

So when my wife, Lauren, asked me afterward, "Matt, you doing okay?" I said, "Yeah. I'm good." But knowing me well enough to dig a bit deeper, she said, "No, Matt, look at me . . . how are you doing?"

I told her—again—that I was fine. And honestly, I thought I was. But she also noticed a tear or two that had welled up into my eyes, tipping her off that maybe "No, I'm all right" wasn't exactly the correct answer from every cavern of my body. So I shouldn't have been too surprised when my friend Josh called me a little while later and said, "Hey, Lauren thought I might should check up on you. She told me you're struggling a little."

Did I feel busted? Set up? Spied on? Embarrassed?

No. Because as hard as I may try to flex out my chest and deny my fears and anxieties, the only place I really want them to live—when they insist on intruding—is out here in the light, where "he is in the light" . . . where He's given us "fellowship with one another" . . . and where "the blood of Jesus his Son" is readily able to remind me that all my worries, as overwhelming as they may seem at the moment, are actually 20,000 years or more out of date. Just think what His peace and prosperity will have proven to me by then.

That's why moments like these are actually clarifying, even in their difficulty. They give us a clearer picture than we usually see of that part of us (our earthly treasure) that is already scheduled for returning to dust, while also giving us opportunity to set our sights on the part of us He will preserve eternally (our heavenly treasure). This takes nothing away from the trouble of today, the losses we experience while living under the curse of the Fall. But we grieve in the loving arms of the Father, in hopeful view of Christ's return, amid the already dawning shadows of the new heavens and the new earth.

Are you feeling afraid today? That's all right.

A little anxious? It's okay. I know.

But I can tell you from personal experience that one of the most merciful acts of God in my life has come from showing me that really—really, Matt?—there's nothing I can do but trust Him. Another plate of spinach is not going to save me. Upping my blueberry intake may be a smart choice, but it won't drive away every unwanted intruder from my bloodstream. I'm wise to be a good steward, but I'll never be my own rescuer.

The worst thing you can do with fear and anxiety is to pretend you're too strong to have them. The best thing you can do is just to let Him be in charge of them.

Because He's in charge anyway.

And in Him, you're in His peace.

That's not just good. That's great.

Chapter 9

Keep On Tugging

Pulling Up Roots, Putting Down Stakes

"My life got a lot harder after that day."

We'll call this Exhibit A. Lest anyone's ever tried to sugarcoat Christianity for you, like it's some kind of family pass to Disneyland—one long fun experience of parade floats and funnel cakes, fantasy rides and photo ops—you can cancel our seats on that cruise line at any time. We're not here to be God's publicity crew or advance men, talking nothing but sweetness and light and $1,000 checks in the mail. So whether you're a Christian confused by the difficulties you're still facing in life, or you're an unconvinced unbeliever who's pretty sure the sinner's prayer is a sales pitch, we give you the nine-word sentence quoted at the top of this page, written by a woman named Michelle, looking back fourteen years to the moment of her conversion. The "that day" she's talking about is *that day*. And to put it in context, the twenty some-odd years beforehand (before her life became, in her words, "a lot harder") included childhood abuse, alcoholism, depression, Prozac, a codependent marriage, a job as a stripper, and a tense moment on her bathroom floor when she begged three paramedics to let her die and go to hell. As far as she was concerned, it sure as heaven couldn't be any worse than *this* place.

But the more you hear and know of the gospel—of the pain and the process that's often involved in freeing us from our sin (on a practical basis, in daily terms)—this confession becomes the honest description of how we're sometimes left to feel. Christian living, taken seriously, is not playtime. It is tough sledding. It doesn't typically follow the screenplay of those testimonials that air on religious TV channels, especially the parts that come after the music modulates and the B-roll brightens into a sunlit picnic and a game of catch in the backyard.

For Michelle, it meant a deep dive into difficult forgiveness, a brick-wall relationship with an unsupportive husband, bouts against longstanding sins and open wounds and other heart issues that refused to go gently into the good night—things that didn't just roll over and vacate the premises once the Holy Spirit moved in. Things that weren't high on her punch list of cool ways to spend the summer.

Hard things.

But over time, the dangers of learning to walk against the headwinds of her own habitual second nature, the discomfort of seeing new shortcomings exposed to the light of truth, the doubts that mocked her sense of worthiness to receive and apply the grace of God—they each became, in His transformative hand, master tools that sprung her loose to enjoy a tangible freedom with Christ. The more spiritual surgeries she underwent, the more healing she experienced, until she increasingly began trusting and more often feeling like the beloved daughter of the Most High that she already was, purified by His blood, exhibiting clear indicators of spiritual fruit such as peace, joy, and love. One of her friends, in fact, who knew her from all the way back to the old days, still says to her, "When you're standing here in front of me, Michelle, I can see that it's you—I remember you—but it's like you're somebody I've never known before."

Change.

God's hardworking change.

It's where the good life comes from.

But it's the *only* place it comes from.

So we want to encourage you, in what perhaps sounds like sort of a roundabout way, not to "lose heart" while the gospel is slowly being renewed in you "day by day" (2 Cor. 4:16). We want to take all the powerful truths we've uncovered so far, as well as the uncomfortable truths we've discovered about ourselves, and drive a stake in the ground that says, "I'm committed to this process that God knows is best for me. I'm surrendering myself for the long haul to whatever tactics of His are meant to draw me all the way into His love and victory . . . more all the time, more each day."

And in order to continue this undertaking, we need something besides a quick fix.

Can't be a silver bullet.

The "silver bullet," you probably know, derives from the mythical folklore of the werewolf. Long ago in certain medieval cultures, if a grisly murder was committed and remained unsolved, remained a mystery, the crime might be attributed to a werewolf— a half-man/half-wolf creature who shape-shifted under a full moon into a raging monster with deadly appetites. But trying to find him and kill him was no easy task. No spring-loaded snare in the grass or an old ordinary weapon was capable of bringing down this rabid purveyor of evil. The only bane of the prowling werewolf was the successful aim of a direct shot—and not with just any kind of explosive strike, but with a special brand of ammo fired from the chamber.

A silver bullet.

Silver bullets, then, are for fantasy action movies—as well as for gullible idiots who think those guys on the infomercials, the ones with the six-pack abs, actually achieved their buff physique by strapping that flimsy, mass-produced, strap contraption thingy around their midsection for as little as six measly seconds a day. ("And if you're one of the next fifty callers, we'll even throw in a matching sports bottle.")

Right.

That's not how it works. You knew that, right? You don't get chiseled abs in six seconds.

Christian maturity either.

Actually, you get it the same way the Mr. Universe ad models got it—through an ongoing ethic, a healthy measure of discipline, a regular regimen of reverse engineering.

And for believers, this means (1) *renouncing* what is old, (2) *rerooting* in what is new, and (3) perpetually *asking* God for help to keep this transformation happening.

"My life got a lot harder after that day," she said.

But one day she looked up and couldn't believe the difference. Neither will you.

Renouncing, Rerooting

Remember today how dead you were before.

If you don't remember, here's the Bible to remind you . . .

You were dead in the trespasses and sins in which you once walked, following the course of this world, following the prince of the power of the air, the spirit that is now at work in the sons of disobedience. (Eph. 2:1–2)

"Were."

"You were."

If you're a Christian, your life was rooted deeply in death before God reached down and remade you. You were out of fellowship with your Creator. Whether you were five or fifty or any nice round age in between or after, you were grounded in dry, malnourished soil, disconnected from God, held down by and predisposed to a fallen heritage of guilt and shame, of fear and anxiety, of selfish ambition and pride, needy cries for approval, worldly cravings, even religious fakery and manipulation.

And some of those roots are tough coming up.

They're the kind of roots that led us into "carrying out the desires of the body and the mind," that led us into bearing the rancid, unpleasant fruit of anger, abuse, self-hate, lust. And as a result of it all, we "were," by the nature of our sin-saturated souls, "children of wrath," the Bible says, "like the rest of mankind" (Eph. 2:3).

All of us. Were.

Yes, objects of God's wrath, simply for breathing His air into our sinful lungs. It wasn't "wrath" like the strike of a lightning bolt or the sudden, crashing rush of a tsunami or tidal wave. It was more like a steadily building opposition, an ever-widening distance between Him and us.

But His wrath, as we humbly know, is tinged with mercy. When we see it on display in Scripture, God's wrath is often seen as He allows people to pursue whatever they want, knowing (of course) it'll be the death of them, but waiting until they finally reach such a confining, desperate, dead end that they cry out for rescue. Such scenes are pictures of creation "subjected to futility." But because of His boundless mercy, it's a creation that's still within sight of the shoreline, that's still within reach of "hope" (Rom. 8:20).

So into this adversarial situation, "God, being rich in mercy, because of the great love with which he loved us, even when we were dead in our trespasses, made us alive together with Christ" (Eph. 2:4–5). We're no longer past tense now; we're past, present, and future. All together. We're on a new, forward trajectory from death to life. And while our spirits were reborn in an instant as a "new creation" (2 Cor. 5:17; Gal. 6:15), while the promise of heaven is as inalterable as His covenant, we know from living experience that conversion is only the beginning of the process that uproots these faulty instincts and attitudes, thereby crimping the fuel lines that send up energy to our sinful behaviors.

Thus, life stays hard.

Because roots often die slowly.

And they don't usually respond to silver bullets.

So if you're struggling mightily today with some of these false paths we've talked about—warped approaches to life that, truthfully, are indicative of idolatry, the furthest thing from being gospel-centered—there's a reason why the pain points of wrestling with your sins and fears are so troubling and upsetting to you. And you ought not despise these difficult experiences that tug on your heart and ache to the core. Because *God's* the one who's doing it. *God's* the one who knows you'll never be whole if the only solution He ever implements in your life is just pruning back the bad behavior. *God's* the one who's either allowing or introducing situations that are putting this kind of pressure on the roots, working to pull up this plant that's destroying you.

"It makes me feel like I'm not saved." No, no. It's actually some of the best evidence of the exact opposite. The struggle to trust Him means He's put new desires in your heart. "Why, though? Why this? Why so hard?" Because He loves you so much. Because He's thinking ten million steps ahead of you—far past this weekend or next fiscal year or the vacation you're planning for summer. He wants you totally free to enjoy and explore whatever's coming up next, to experience it all as a connected part of your life with Him, not to be bound up with hindrances and secrets that cheat you from being fully yourself and fully alive in every moment. Beyond that, He wants to bless the generations that follow you with love and life and low, low levels of carry-on baggage. And the more ruthlessly He gardens, way down into the depths of your heart, the more unlikely the roots underneath your kids and grandkids will be packed down hard and nearly impossible to sever.

So that's why the Holy Spirit's hands are clasped around some of those jumbo roots in your life, the ones that feel like their tendrils must be embedded down into the bedrock, or perhaps running clear through to the other side of the world. And yes, it hurts to feel them tearing and splintering. Hurts even more when we're resisting and tugging back from the other end. But there's no other way to keep these roots from growing out into scrubby, unsightly underbrush than for Him to yank on them firmly enough until even the tiniest extremity is up and out of the ground.

So don't despise it.

Renounce the root, but not the Gardener.

And replant yourself into gospel ground, where new, sanctified roots can grow into much more delicious fruit.

"Well, I don't care, I'm sick of this," you may say. Yeah, we get that. "Seems like He could ease off on me a little, cut me some slack." But just speaking for the two of us, both of whom have a long run of Christian life behind us—long enough that some of these misplaced roots should be thoroughly composted into dark, wormy dirt by now—old plants still pop up out of nowhere and surprise us with how thick they've grown. "Man! I thought I'd gotten rid of that sin. I was already on to the next thing." We can't *believe* sometimes that we're dealing with this one particular problem again. But showing us what we're still capable of producing from roots that aren't grounded fully in Him and in His truth is not only God's way of being wisely challenging toward us, but also of loving us—loving us too much to let things go, where they can continue to hurt us, continue to hurt others, and continue to keep us from glorifying Him with our improbable obedience.

These roots, again (just to be clear) are the desires of our hearts. And the problem is not the fact that they're present—the fact that we have desires. The problem is where we're seeking to plant them, where we're rooting them. If we root them in the kingdom of the world—in earthly things and pursuits that cannot satisfy—these roots have no other choice but to spring up as bad fruit (addictions, anxiety, depression, abuse, misappropriated anger, and so forth). But if we root these same desires in the kingdom of heaven—in the truths and promises of God—they will instead produce the fruit of the Spirit within us (love, joy, peace, patience, kindness, goodness, faithfulness, gentleness, self-control—Gal. 5:22–23). They will keep us planted under the waterfall of grace that's afforded us through the gospel of Jesus Christ.

Not only that, but "in the coming ages" He's going to show us even *more* loving reasons why this choice to serve Him as our king was worth it and why He put so much investment into us, things we won't possibly be able to understand until He reveals to us throughout eternity the "immeasurable riches of his grace" and the astounding kindness that was riding behind all His activity toward us (Eph. 2:7).

So in the meantime, we employ the ongoing ethic of *renouncing* who we once were—those traits and reflexes that can still seem so natural and justifiable to us—while constantly *rerooting* ourselves in the gospel promise that "we are his workmanship" (could actually read, "we are his *poetry*"), "created in Christ Jesus for good works, which God prepared beforehand, that we should walk in them" (Eph. 2:10). You "put off your old self, which belongs to your former manner of life and is corrupt through deceitful desires," and you instead become "renewed in the spirit of your minds," putting on "the new self, created after the likeness of God in true righteousness and holiness" (Eph. 4:22–24).

That's who we "are."

We *were* dead in our trespasses and sins. We *were* following the course and pattern of this world. We *were* by our very nature an object of God's wrath.

But God made us alive with Him.

And that means it's always the right season to be planting.

Asking for Directions

Day by day. An ongoing ethic.

Not a silver bullet, but a true relationship.

A common phrase found in Paul's writings from Scripture are the words "once and for all." Thank God that so many glorious aspects of the gospel and His merciful favor toward us are each "once and for all."

But this renouncing and rerooting business is not "once and for all." It's day by day, whereby "our outer self is wasting away" and "our inner self is being renewed" (2 Cor. 4:16). And one of the reasons why God manages the process in this manner is because it keeps us asking of Him, keeps us pleading. It keeps us from running off independently where we'd only succeed at getting too big for our britches, forgetting that every blessing of the gospel is the result of being hidden in Christ, being identified with God.

So the asking becomes a daily, ongoing experience as well—of admitting need and being with Him. Of repenting and receiving, of confessing and changing. We don't get bogged down in last year's struggles, nor worry about how long we'll continue to be so subject to the same temptations (which, by the way, is not sin, but sure can feel like it). We just focus on winning the day. That's the objective. *Win the day.* And we keep walking through it and into it, day after trusting day, thanking Him for not leaving a stone unturned that might block us from enjoying all of Him.

Because actually, the truth of the matter is, life is going to be hard anyway. Hate to break it to you like that. Whether *with* Christ, or *without* Christ—despite plenty of good times and reasons to celebrate—there's much to not be overly thrilled about in the future. You weary Christians who are tired of still struggling, and you others who see Christianity as a burden you don't need to carry right now, just need to realize that life becomes hard for everybody, in one way or another.

But when you near your final days before slipping off into eternity, with the strain of life still jiggling a few more tugs on your root system, do you want to be worn out with nothing to show for it, or do you want to feel worked out and rejuvenated by what God has done to transform you?

"Michelle, I can see that it's you—I remember you—but it's like you're somebody I've never known before."

That's somebody who's better for the struggle, who's growing more like Christ by being His worshiper at all costs.

Chapter 10

Go in Peace

Reconciling and Amending

Ask any group of people whether or not they've individually sinned against, hurt, or wounded another person in some way in the past twelve to eighteen months, and nearly every hand in the room will go up. For example, in a crowd of 5,000 or so at our campus in Flower Mound, Texas—each responding to that question one Sunday morning—a solid 85 percent raised their hands (eyes closed) to say yes. Factoring in the 10 percent or more who absolutely hate those "raise your hand" things in church or in public—who wouldn't raise their hand if asked, "Do you have a right hand?"—plus the percentage of folks who rarely if ever admit their own faults and who sure wouldn't tell *you*, even if they did—and we're suddenly getting very close to a one-to-one ratio. Practical unanimity.

Unscientific, we know, but it still doesn't take a mathematical genius to extrapolate a fairly safe hypothesis: If you're more than about six years old and possess the mental faculties to be reading this book, you too would almost certainly be one who'd say, "Yeah, that includes me. I've done that. I've sinned against someone, maybe even recently, and not taken any real steps to apologize or make it right."

It's all of us.

Deducing it is not "rocket surgery," as they say.

And so that means within the next week or two—if we're serious about this—in homes and coffee shops and office parks and restaurants everywhere, thousands of people like you (and us) could be arranging sit-downs with other people in our lives, and potentially removing enormous obstacles from those relationships, not to mention a nagging disturbance from our own conscience. More importantly, we'd be part of reflecting what's meant to be a hallmark of the gospel: "By this all people will know that you are my disciple," Jesus said, "if you have love for one another" (John 13:35).

The results could be phenomenal.

Spiritually, kingdom-wide incredible.

But you don't just go plowing into these choppy waters unprepared. In fact, that's why we've deliberately arranged the material of this book in the exact order we've presented it—because until we realize through Christ that we've been fully pardoned, declared innocent, accepted without reservation as a delighted-in child by the Father, and have been given a means of legitimately removing the burden of our guilt and shame, our fear and anxiety, our anger, abuse, lust, and rebellion, then we're not realistically at a place of freedom to seek or risk another's forgiveness.

The Golden Rule provides a good, concise example of what we're talking about. The greatest commandment, Jesus said, is to "love the Lord your God" with all your heart, soul, strength, and mind, "and your neighbor as yourself" (Luke 10:27). And there's a reason for this sequence, why one comes before the other. Any trouble we may be experiencing in loving others—the second part of Jesus' statement here—is first an indication that something is not squared up in our loving relationship with God. If reconciliation with other people is ever going to be genuine, not meant to prove a point but simply to demonstrate the love of Christ and the transformation He's brought about in our hearts, then we must first be vertically aligned and at rest in Him. We must know how completely loved we are, and must overflow with loving gratitude for the grace and forgiveness He's given us through salvation.

No, being reconciled to God doesn't make us suddenly immune from sinning against others—nor of being sinned against *by* others (a not-so-subtle tease for the next chapter). But the recovery of redemption does mean that even the way we deal with these horizontal difficulties of life has been thoroughly redeemed through the gospel.

So get ready.

There's even *more* freedom out there for you in your future.

Terms of Engagement

You'll remember, thinking back to the early chapters, how we talked about the four general categories of crooked paths we all walk, in hopes of attempting redemption. Before we're saved, we're basically confined to one or all of these four doomed strategies. And even those of us who've received Christ as Savior often go back to dabbling in them at various points along the way. Remember what they were?

We look to *ourselves*, trying to be good enough.

To *others*, seeking their approval and acceptance.

To the *world*, hoping it'll keep our tank filled up.

Even to *religion*, turning faith into a game we play.

But among the hazards involved (many of which we've already addressed) in messing with these dry, spotty wells, another whole classification of problems crops up around the area of our relationships. For example, if we're dead set on putting all our energies into creating better versions of ourselves, becoming a stout enough "us" until we think we've really made it in life, aren't we almost forced to use others as leverage to help us get there? Does it not require using other people as commodities that we assemble and employ for our own purposes? We may succeed at getting them to tell us how great we are, to do what we want them to do. But is that any real way to cultivate friendships? Is that a healthy, helpful way to lead or interact within a family? To run a business? To do our jobs? Won't we invariably leave behind a pile of bruised, hurt, discarded bodies if our first devotion is primarily to the cult of self?

We could go on and on, looking at any of the other four options . . . because they all follow the same progression. Every bum trail we take will cause a rash of collateral damage, littering our whole lives with people that we've asked too much of, taken advantage of, gotten tired of, and become insanely jealous of. We'll grow bitter, angry, resentful, frustrated, overbearing, distrustful, unforgiving, disappointed.

In other words, we'll sin against other people.

There's no other way around it.

Anytime we're not converting to others the same glorious realities that sealed our *own* redemption in Christ, we're always an inch or less away from doing something wicked to somebody else—from not listening to them, not caring about them, not working hard for them, not valuing them, and all the various, ugly expressions that our lack of real love can embody. We won't give people the benefit of the doubt. We won't feel inclined to be gracious. We'll all too quickly assume our attack positions, establishing ourselves on a war footing. We'll flare up at perceived injustices and fight back with counterstrikes. We'll turn against people. We'll do it all. And know we're doing it. And sometimes, we won't even care.

But God, in times like these, in one of those somewhat uncomfortable intrusions of His grace, will very faithfully lean a nudging pressure on us, a healthy weight that implies necessary action, almost like a father exerting a gentle hand on the small of his little child's back, propelling him forward to go apologize to his friend or to the shop owner he took a candy bar from.

Our Father is like that. The One who pursued us in making peace also desires that we respond to others in kind . . .

By pursuing peace.

And if we properly understand and want to be shaped by His gospel, we'll approach what this process asks of us from an entirely different perspective than before. Rather than becoming an expert in other people's sins while staying ignorant of our own, rather than working to make sure we get the better end of the deal without tarnishing our reputations, we'll take our offenses seriously and concern ourselves with magnifying God's character through our lives rather then fighting to preserve our pretend dignity.

We'll do it His way.

Think of it in terms of *authority*. You would never say in response to a police officer who'd pulled you over, "What, you're telling me to stay in my car? Why don't you go back and get in *your* car, let me come up there and ask *you* a few questions." You would never answer your boss by demanding, "Here, let me tell you how we're going to run this company. I'll tell you how many hours I'm going to work, I'll tell you what time I show up in the morning, I'll tell you how much money you'll pay me, and I'll tell you what'll happen if you don't do what I'm saying." That's obviously not the way it goes. The one who's *under* authority in these tense situations takes a back seat, and the one who's *in* authority assumes responsibility for how things should play out.

Whenever believers are involved in conflict with other people, God remains the authority—not us. He's in charge of orchestrating what needs to happen next for His own kingdom good. Therefore, what He wants to accomplish in bringing us back into good terms with the people we've harmed or injured in some way is of supreme importance compared to our own desire for justifying ourselves, or reaching a settlement, or forging a new understanding about what we expect this other person to do or feel going forward.

Look, He just wants us pursuing peace.

The way *He* pursues peace.

Romans 12:18—"If possible, so far as it depends on you, live peaceably with all."

If the gospel's not involved in resolving these clashes, if we don't care what God's wanting, then sure, it can be all about the money. It can be all about the principle of the matter. It can be all about our own plans for how we wanted to spend the weekend or whose house we want to go to for Christmas. It can be all about winning, about unloading on somebody, about proving ourselves right with point-by-point fake bullet points.

But with the gospel in place, the "love of Christ compels us" (2 Cor. 5:14 HCSB), in view of His own sacrificial mercies toward us, to no longer measure people and our encounters with them "according to the flesh" (v. 16), as though what matters most in this boxing match is whatever title belt we're each fighting over.

No. Nothing of "the flesh" matters anymore. Not to believers. The gospel gets us way past that. All the old stuff we wanted to gain in our jockeying with others came from *us*, from our own little snits and pouts, from our moody, grumpy, self-absorbed hearts. From now on, however, "All this is from God, who through Christ *reconciled* us to himself and gave us the *ministry of reconciliation*" (v. 18).

We're after something totally different now.

And it totally changes the way we say "I'm sorry."

Vision Correction

Cognitive therapy presents us with the concept of a *schema* (pronounced SKEE-ma), which refers to the lens through which we view the world. Put both hands six inches in front of your face, lay your fingers at an angle against each other to form sort of a goalie's mask or honeycomb, and you're looking out on life through the rubric of your own sights, memories, and interpretations. You're taking in what you want to take in, and leaving out what you want to leave out. You're seeing it through your own grid.

That's why, when two or more people recollect a commonly observed event—like what happened in the car that night, or what was said after he said what she said and they said—the resulting diaries will rarely read the exact same way. *That went well, don't you think?* versus *No, that was the worst night of my life!*

Same crime scene, multiple reports.

And if something occurred during this interaction that caused feelings to be hurt or sides to be taken, you can be sure—of the global super-set that encompasses all the liability for what happened—the breakdown of blame will be distributed in some measure among the participants. If not 50–50, more like 60–40, 75–25. But *hardly ever*—and we say this from long experience, both as husbands and fathers, also as pastors and counselors who've walked with numerous people through all kinds of war zones—*hardly ever* is it one-sided, a hundred to nothing. Child abuse, incest, rape—we'd all probably agree on the extreme examples where these same conclusions wouldn't exactly apply. But in the vast majority of life interactions, we each bring our share of responsibility into the mix.

True, one of the combatants may have done considerably less to start the fire or stir the pot. They may have handled themselves very patiently and honorably considering what went down. But typically they did do *something.* The percentage on their side of the equation may be calculated in the single digits to low teens— nothing much more than a chilly reception perhaps—but it does register on the thermometer. And 20 percent of sin, even when dwarfed by somebody else's 80 percent, is still sin.

And our sin distorts (Jer. 17:9).

"Well, I wouldn't have done what I did if he hadn't . . . if she hadn't . . ." Right, we think half the verses in the Bible are marked by little asterisks, keyed to a disclaimer at the bottom that reads, "Except you" or "Except when somebody really acts up on you." We can rationalize away any behavior on our part by appealing to an exemption based on what somebody else did to set us off. "What am I supposed to do, God, when somebody like this is working against me all the time?"

Well, looks like He's already *shown* us what He would do: initiate and forgive, engage and reconcile, pursue peace at all costs.

Why should it be any different in our case?

That's why Matthew 7 is the customary landing area for biblical conflict management and personal responsibility. It's the old log-and-speck analogy (vv. 3–5), where Jesus picks up on our tendency to obsess over the obscure flaws in our opponent—"the speck that is in your brother's eye"—while the whole time a redwood tree is embedded in our *own* eye. A little gross, maybe, yet a lot true.

But if you've heard this New Testament passage enough times that it's almost lost the ability to affect you, follow us back to less familiar territory in Ezekiel 14, where God is speaking to one of His major prophets. The people of Israel, the Lord said, had taken "idols into their hearts" and had set "the stumbling block of their iniquity before their faces" (v. 3). What, then, should He do when these people come to Him, or when they come to one of the prophets, wanting to know how the Lord will counsel them or direct them or lead them through various issues in their lives where they're needing help?

Actually, here's a better question. How well should these people expect to see the face of God or the light of His Word at all if they'd deliberately parked an idol in their blind spot, a "stumbling block" composed entirely of their own unrepentant sins? What kind of divine directions should they expect to follow if they couldn't even see well enough to know where His voice was coming from?

These stumbling blocks of iniquity—these things we value, love, even idolize—skew our ability to see rightly, and then cause us to make decisions based on those distortions. We should never expect to be able to grasp God's will or see clearly enough to know how to react wisely amid our relational struggles if we're peering through a maze of sin to find out.

So God said, before He'd do anything, He first needed to "lay hold of the hearts of the house of Israel," because they'd become "estranged" from Him by placing their own iniquities between themselves and God (v. 5). They'd allowed a pile of crates to stack up in their front yard, blockages that would only continue to prevent them from knowing or following God's lead as long they refused to let Him deal with the clutter, letting Him bust it up and clear it out of the way . . . thereby eliminating the estrangement.[2]

What this tells us is very important: that we're actually sinning against God when we let these logs (or even our own specks!) continue to pile up. And before they've finished doing damage, they will have led us repeatedly into pride and self-protection, distancing us from brothers and sisters, wives and husbands, parents and in-laws, and whatever other people we could personally name that we've mistreated, misused, or misunderstood.

Leave it to none other than the book of Numbers (of all places) to bring out the consistency of this connection. God says . . .

> When a man or woman commits any of the sins that people commit by breaking faith with the LORD, and that person realizes his guilt, he shall confess his sin that he has committed. [Then watch this:] And he shall make full restitution for his wrong, adding a fifth to it and *giving it to him to whom he did the wrong.* (Num. 5:6–7, emphasis added)

How interesting. The person's sin in this instruction is described as "breaking faith with the LORD." The infraction is against God. But our various sins, by their concentric nature, inevitably ripple out and create havoc in our relationships. Therefore, we can never disregard God without also disturbing our peace and unity with others. The consequences always go wider than the boundaries of our own hearts. So our reaction to recognized sin, the Lord says—beyond just confessing it privately to Him— needs also to involve the regular practice of going to people we've impacted through our disobedience, and making proper restitution for our offense—no, even "adding a fifth to it." Bringing extra. Showing by the seriousness and extravagance of our humble desire that we are intent on making peace.

And only a heart transformed by God would do that.

The reconciliation He's brought about for us, when well examined and understood, begins to beat out a new rhythm in our heart, a joyful celebration of His undeserved grace and mercy. But it's a rhythm that should bebop all the way down into our feet, swinging our dance of fellowship with Him out onto the hardwood floor, places where we've been involved in various scrapes and incidents that have separated friends and families, where we've let others down and broken their hearts. In this way, the rhythm of reconciliation becomes one fluid motion of vertical worship and a quest for horizontal unity. And before you know it, the music of the gospel is doing what it always does.

The gospel changes things.

Imagine the Possibilities

But what about when it doesn't seem to change *anything*? What do we do when they won't forgive?

Here's the hard reality. Sin, sort of like a municipal building project, is almost always more costly than people think or expect it to be. The overruns can go deep and bleed red. And when we sin against others and create discord, we forfeit the ability to determine how deep a gash it inflicts. Therefore, even our most humble, genuine expression of regret is always susceptible to being shrugged off, rebuffed, or sent angrily packing. To borrow from the terminology of the last chapter, our pleas for forgiveness are not silver bullets. They can fail to achieve the desired results.

And we've just got to be okay with that . . . because that's more than we can control. We must sometimes accept the minimum goal of our peacemaking efforts (at least temporarily) as the maximum payoff. We can't demand reciprocity or guarantee a hug/handshake at the end.

But . . .

We can make triple sure that we're coming to this confession with a heart that's fully repentant and confident in God's forgiveness, with our only aim the prayer that we can establish peace with this person, if peace indeed can be won.

1. We can own it. We can give 100 percent on our part for every percentage point of sin we've committed—and then some. We can look inside ourselves for fault, down to the very thoughts in our own head and the motivations that led us to deal cowardly or unkindly with another. We may only (or primarily) be guilty of reacting badly to what this person did, whether by flashing a frustrated temper or withholding our interest and affection toward them. But with the gospel at our back, we can own every bit of whatever we did, taking full responsibility for it.

2. We can avoid all accusations. The boiler-plate script for relational conflict calls for everybody to think the other person is more to blame for what happened. So if you somehow long to feel like a fourth grader on the playground again, just let yourself descend to the lowest common denominator of life's most common disagreements. "Well, *you* started it!" "No, *you* started it!" "No, you!" "No, you!" Lord, help us not ever give voice to such childishness again. Instead, may we come to these interactions saying, "I'm not accusing you of anything or asking you for anything except your forgiveness." That's it. Case closed.

3. We can make no excuses. No ifs, buts, or maybes. No trying to build makeshift platforms for our sins on the stilts of another person's words or actions. No judging our own righteousness based on the terms of what someone else did, but rather on the holy, unchangeable standards of God. Instead, we specifically name what we've done, we acknowledge the pain and difficulty we've introduced into their lives, and we leave the ball tenderly in their court, fully realizing they can take whatever time necessary to accept our apology and hopefully help us rebuild what we've contributed in breaking.

But if, despite our clear conscience and authentic intentions, the person with whom we're trying to make amends either doesn't believe us or wants no part of what we're trying to reconcile with them, the Scriptures leave us but one holy and wise alternative: to bless them and move on . . . and continue to pray and hold ourselves accountable for being consistent and true toward them. We'll keep learning what we can learn, and we'll keep hoping they'll one day be able to release *themselves* from the torments that unforgiveness can inflict. And when that day finally comes—if it does—our cheerful, relieved gratitude will have remained just as fresh and loving toward them as if they'd forgiven us right on the spot.

Relationships can't always be restored fully on this side of heaven, but it is no indictment on the gospel when we make that admission—because in Christ, there are no longer any such things as irreconcilable differences. Whenever restoration fails to take place, it's because someone on either side of the equation isn't grabbing hold of the promises God has made. They're not willing to cut loose and start singing the song of redemption.

Therefore "if possible"—which tells us sometimes it's not—"so far as it depends on you"—which says they may never counter your plea with the answer you're wanting—"live peaceably with all"—which means it's probably time you started talking.

Raise your hand, and reconciliation will call on you.

Chapter II

Feel the Heartburn

Confronting and Forgiving

Maybe it was the soy vodka lattes she brought with her to Sunday school. Maybe it was the smell of alcohol on her breath, already present at lunch. And so maybe she should've seen it coming. But when Kristine's friend Brenda confronted her one afternoon about her drinking problem, she was quick with the "how dare yous" and "you just don't understand"—"you have no earthly idea what you're talking about or what I've been through in life."

She'd actually been drinking since she was twelve, and had been using it as self-medication throughout high school and college, trying to quiet the noisy demons of sexual abuse, shame, and disappointment. But it would be a cold day in Honolulu before she ever gave Brenda the time of day again—as well as Brenda's husband, Tom, who taught the singles class at church and also counseled her on Friday mornings.

People living under downtown bridges were the ones with "drinking problems," not people like Kristine. She had a job—a *good* job, thank you, in the corporate accounting industry—an apartment, a new car, money in the bank, friends. Did she drink? Yeah. No big secret there. But was it a problem? Come on. *Give me a break.*

But let's cut away from this narrative, and catch up with Kristine again a number of months later. An ordinary weekday. Early in the morning. 7:00. Getting ready for work, and yet her thoughts were already buzzing, even as she was bustling around the house, putting herself together. Her denial and indignation over Brenda's bald-faced charges had hardly cooled a single degree, perhaps even growing a little warmer as the weeks had passed. The same feelings, the same defenses, the same defiant resentment over being so directly accused, were all swirling around in her head. Or . . . wait . . . was the swirling sensation actually coming from . . . from the drink in her hand? The one that had become so much of a breakfast fixture in her life that she'd almost stopped noticing it as being unusual, out of the ordinary?

It's 7:00.

And I'm drinking.

Who starts drinking at 7:00 unless . . .

She called Brenda that day. And said Brenda was right. *Of course,* she was right. And maybe Tom was even right, who had taken the liberty of making her an appointment for inpatient treatment at a local hospital. Didn't mean Kristine was yet totally finished kicking against them—screaming, punching, cussing, crying, resisting their appeal for her to seek such radical help for her "problem." But when the doctor took her by the arm, wanting

to make sure she was listening to what her blood work was saying—telling her she would not survive the raging hepatitis in her
liver for another five years if she continued on with her drinking
habit—she realized her godly friends weren't out to lambaste her
but to love her.

Had they hurt her feelings? Yes. Badly. Had they stabbed her
in the heart? Yes. With blunt honesty. And twisted it till it hurt.
But is she alive in Christ today because of faithful friends who
cared enough to confront what was actively killing her?

Let's just say the gospel's a lot tougher than we think.

Fight or Flight?

The vast majority of us are old hands at avoiding conflict.[3]
We've gathered from our various experiences in life that the risk
of bad things happening in response to hard, honest conversations
usually makes them not worth the effort of initiating. Ever. They
feel wrong. They sound mean. All we'll end up doing is causing
ourselves a lot of stress, discomfort, nerves, and awkward silences,
only to most likely be tagged as the enemy when everything's said
and done.

And to a degree, we may be right to steer away from the
majority of these confrontations, especially those that deal with
sins we've directly incurred from others. It is our "glory," the Bible
says, "to overlook an offense" (Prov. 19:11). One of the marks of
Christian maturity is a willingness to absorb and forgive any ugli-
ness or injustice that's tossed in our direction, and to let our desire
for retaliation or rebuttal fall peaceably to the ground. A "soft
answer" is the wise, biblical strategy for dialing down the potential

buildup of animosity and moving on to a more conducive use for our energy and attention (Prov. 15:1).

But there are ways to tell when healthy deflection has morphed into utter denial, when instead of living in trustful dependence on God and with a desire for John 13, gospel-inspired peace and unity with others, we're being driven instead by fear and pride and anger and self-centeredness and a noticeable tolerance for free-floating division.

One of those warning signs is when we begin to detect in our hearts what the Bible calls a "root of bitterness" (Heb. 12:15)— when we can tell we're just getting really frustrated and peevish with somebody, when we're losing the ability to interact with them without kinda hating their guts or at least thinking very unfriendly things about them.

Now bitterness—obviously—isn't a glowing testament to our character. The fact that it's slow-burning inside of us is no one's fault but our own. It makes up part of the percentage of overall blame that we'll need to take personal ownership for. To repent of. But let's not act like bitterness is not a real, fallback emotion, as though it's beyond our Christian capabilities of harboring. Because, yes, it can lodge there. And if we let it keep flaming up without doing anything about it, we're just denying something that has the potential (according to the rest of that verse from Hebrews 12) to spring up and cause a lot of trouble, "and by it many become defiled."

Bitterness is a powder keg. Pay attention to it.

It can mean we're denying what sin is doing to us. Not just *our* sin, but also *their* sin.

A second indicator of unhealthy conflict avoidance is when our knee-jerk reaction to relational difficulty is to run away from the problem, becoming what we might describe as a "flighter"—which is probably not a real word, but we think it gets the message across. Flighters simply remove themselves from uncomfortable or upsetting situations where they're being hurt, whether it be a church, a job, a relationship, even their marriage. But as proof of how ineffective this denial tactic almost always is, notice how often it becomes a repeated pattern, a reflex, something that becomes more easily justified with each new opportunity for choosing it. Flighters, before long, will run from one church to another, from one group of friends to another, from one source of disharmony to another, until they've run through all their relationships and *still* haven't found a place where people don't have the access to upset or disappoint them.

That's because sin is the native language in every zip code. And the minute you move in, one more sinner just showed up. If you think you can avoid all clashes with others by constantly staying on the move, looking for the perfect place where nobody is ever in a position to rile or offend you, you'll be chasing that myth all over the world and never finding it. Because no place like that actually exists.

Only in the mind of a conflict avoider.

On the other end of the spectrum from *avoidant* responses, of course, are *aggressive* responses, folks who almost go out looking to be ticked off, who are so prickly toward others' actions, they've practically never met a motive they couldn't distrust. These are your bullies, your gossips, your grudge-holders, your Bible thumpers. They don't just want to take somebody on, they want to take somebody down. So whereas the most extreme form of conflict *avoidance* might be, let's say, suicide—removing yourself completely from another person's ability to harm you anymore—the most extreme forms of *aggression* would be things like violence and abuse, making people pay for what they've done to you by just punishing them relentlessly, and never having any intention of letting up. *You hurt me? That'll cost you.*

Avoidance. Aggression. Perhaps, as you've been reading, you've been able to plot yourself somewhere along this continuum.

But there's a beautiful little, biblical niche reserved only for gospel-style seating, a place where you can spare yourself the discomfort of dancing around in avoidance and passiveness, or—if retaliation is more your style—stop yourself before your face wrenches up again into vengeance and aggression.

Ephesians 4:15 calls it "speaking the truth in love."

If you've been around Christian vocabulary very much, you've probably heard this turn of phrase before. You recognize the ideal balance conveyed in those five positive, healthy, redemptive-sounding words. But the reason why there's so much gospel embedded in this concept is not because of the truth-speaking dynamic alone, but because of what this verse goes on to identify as the goal or result of this bold, compassionate undertaking. The central purpose of "speaking the truth in love," Paul said, is so that we might "grow up in every way into him who is the head, into Christ."

So when we bring something of concern to a brother or sister's attention, or when they courageously point out to us a matter of sin in our own lives, the leading edge of this border crossing is not a fault-finding objective, but rather a desire to help each other mature in relationship with Jesus.

We said in the last chapter that when we go to someone as a believer to seek that person's forgiveness, the gospel motivates us not to get caught up in defending ourselves or winning an argument, but to be concerned primarily with restoring peace—the way God the Father has restored peace to us through the blood of Jesus Christ.

And the same kind of principle also remains in force when confronting others in their own sin—not to build an airtight case against them or to exert some kind of superior, spiritual control over them, but primarily to exhort them toward joy and harmony in their faith. It's not about being right, catching them red-handed, throwing the net of "aha!" justice around their necks, but rather a proactive love that says, "I am not willing for you to live at the mercy of things that are devilishly designed to destroy you." As we'll see in just a second when we begin walking through Matthew 18, we have nothing more to gain from conversations like these than the return of our brother or sister (v. 15). That's the only win we're after.

So it's obviously not an *aggression* play—not if we're trying to stay biblical and gospel-centered. God in His mercy deals with our sins for the very same reasons: because they are many, and because He is love. Not to shame us. Not to manipulate us. No carrot sticks or litmus tests for earning His reluctant approval.

But much more often than we must guard ourselves against excessive aggression, the call of Christian fellowship means blowing past our naturally tentative *avoidance*—not because we enjoy these altercations or the asking of hard questions, but because we know from our own tough-knocks experience that sin begets sin. Sin builds on itself. And if left unchallenged and unaccounted for by those of us who love these people and who value their souls, we leave them much more susceptible to veering off into places that no right-minded believer would ever want to go.

Cheap love is the kind that avoids, just as cheap love is the kind that pounces and punches and pummels and piles on. *Real* love—even though it's likely to get sick to its stomach, even though it might chomp through a full roll of Tums beforehand, even though it'd rather take a shot to the solar plexus than to do what it's about to do—still goes ahead and does it anyway.

It swallows hard and speaks the truth.

And speaks it in love.

Truth in the Trenches

This subject is so un-American, isn't it? Most of us have cut our teeth on the principles of personal liberty. Individualism. National sovereignty. Neighborhood zoning restrictions. We don't want people in our business, just like we don't want orange barrels and bulldozers in our backyard. Leave us alone, move along, watch your step, and keep your hands out of our Happy Meals.

But the kingdom of God wasn't born on the fourth of July. Neither is it built on the backs of freestylers and entrepreneurial types who dance to their own tune and never take no for an answer. The church is a united, sharing, cooperative organism. A family. A composite of redemptive relationships. And the gospel that forms its connective tissue will always resist the limitations of the big room and the safe distance. Just as the gospel calls us to God, it also calls us to each other.

And because none of us scores a ten in all aspects of Christian living—despite whatever our Facebook postings and Sunday appearances might lead others to believe—we should not be surprised when inconsistencies surface (in all of us) that are harmful to ourselves, our families, our testimony, and our mission. Nor should we be naïve or muzzled enough to think we have no obligation to address certain issues of offense in others, both for the purpose of our own forgiveness of them, as well as the good of everyone involved, not to mention the glory of Christ.

Still, you may say, *sounds to me like an arrogant posture for people to take*. Well, only if your chief goal in life is to avoid making waves, or if the only person's feelings you really care about are yours—or if you somehow believe small talk and fake niceness are preferable to honest, authentic relationships. Because as it turns out, there's more than one reason for getting those Matthew 7 logs out of your eyes. For not only does removing them help you deal directly with some of your own obvious areas of sin and need, but it also helps you "see clearly to take the speck out of your brother's eye" (v. 5).

With gospel unity comes gospel responsibility.

And so here comes our need for Matthew 18.

> "If your brother sins against you, go and tell him his fault, between you and him alone. If he listens to you, you have gained your brother. But if he does not listen to you, take one or two others along with you, that every charge may be established by two or three witnesses. If he refuses to listen to them, tell it to the

church. And if he refuses to listen to the church, let him
be to you as a Gentile and a tax collector." (vv. 15–17)

There are lots of books, lots of teaching and sermon series out there that delve into the methodology and progression of this biblical model for conflict resolution. The Scripture text is straight from the mouth of Jesus, so it represents His expressed instruction for how relational sins and offenses should be handled in the life of the church.

But rather than drill down into steps and specifics that others have covered in ample detail elsewhere (such as in *The Peacemaker*, as mentioned in our endnotes at the back of the book), we just want to share quickly what we've observed and experienced from our own seats at the particular church where we serve.

You're going to think we couldn't possibly enlist a term like "conservatively speaking" to label what we're about to say, but we would estimate that the number of these conversations that have occurred within our membership probably runs into the hundreds of thousands. That's right, six figures. Boatloads. And of that enormous amount of activity, all of it centered around the edifying interplay between God's people—just right here in this one church body—we'd guess that more than 90 percent of these confrontational encounters have never needed to continue beyond the first cup of coffee. By the grace of God, and by the visible mountain of evidence we've seen, we can say with well-reasoned certainty that most people—when challenged in a humble, loving manner, free of personal agenda and vendetta—will hear, repent, confess, and seek restoration.

They'll see what you mean.

And they'll want to change.

Now maybe not immediately. The shock of sincerity may require a little time to sink in. But before any more feelings get hurt, before any additional inquiries need to be made, the road to relational healing usually begins taking hopeful shape at that moment.

It's a thing of heartburn and beauty.

And so what distresses our souls as men who adore the body of Christ is that this promise of healing can exist at such high levels of likelihood, and yet most people will still refuse to touch it with a ten-foot pole. Think of the number of caustic relationships and painful sin patterns that are allowed to stumble forward unobstructed when they could be so effectively sutured and sewn back up in as little as one visit of biblical obedience.

Can it really be that clean? Yes.

Is it always like that? Obviously not.

But for every long, drawn-out, and difficult experience—the ones that may end up with somebody flipping you a bird and storming out of your life for now, if not forever—there are many, many more where the other person appreciates your concern and wants to make it right. Once you can get past the agony of rehearsing your speech and imagining their response, you're likely to find yourself going to bed that night, thinking, *You know? That was worth it. I think I did the right thing.*

Hard. But good. Better.

But when it *doesn't* happen like that, when you go to bed afterward feeling even more upset than you did the night before, the Bible thankfully provides a roadmap that keeps tugging everyone toward the goal of gaining back relationship as brother or sister. It may get messy before it clears up. It may remain ugly and *never* clear up. But because the goal is not just to get it off your chest but to labor for the restored heart of the other person, you cannot just quit and write them off—not until they've given you no other option.

This may surprise you, and it may sound heavy-handed, but we take this responsibility very seriously at our church. We're a covenant community. We've all pledged before God and before each other—in writing—that we will submit ourselves to the teaching of the Word and to the leadership of the church. Obviously, we're each very imperfect in the execution. We all need one another to help hold us accountable and to block the exit ramps when necessary. And when others do, our most healthy response to it—even if we disagree or want to argue back—is to assume there's probably some truth to what they're saying, and to trust that God will purge any impurities to the surface as we kneel before Him and walk this out with our fellow believers. Doesn't mean they're *entirely* right about us, necessarily, but we're wise not to dismiss it without checking our hearts and checking around to see if others might give us the same, objective observation.

So, yes, it's good and wholesome—and ought to be expected—when others point out a failing of ours, or when they spur us on to be more careful, or even when they express personal hurt over something we've done to them or neglected to do for them. Two-way street here. Them to us. We to them. And hopefully, the result is always an apology or a heartfelt thank-you—a genuine reaction of repentance.

But if all we ever get back in return for the painful persistence of our love is something like, "I don't care what you say (or what the Bible says, or what the elders say), you're crazy, you're full of it, just get out of my face"—then we put enough trust in the wisdom of Scripture to follow it through to its gospel end.

And to remove them from fellowship.

That's no way to grow a church. Oh, yes, it is. Because, first of all, our mission is not to grow as big as we can. And second of all, perhaps the greatest, most eternal disservice we can do to another person, and thereby to the integrity of the church, is to watch them steadily rejecting the lordship of Christ while play-acting like they're Christians.

Because, no, they're not.

They're not acting like believers. And Jesus seems to instruct us to treat those who choose their sin over their Savior as those who are not saved.

[Whoa.]

May need to pull your socks back up after that one, but we don't know any other biblical conclusion to draw. Being baptized somewhere as a kid, but then showing no transformation of life, no willingness to walk in obedience to God, no acceptance of a greater authority than the autonomous tyrant of their own will, and yet still expecting to be hailed as a Christian—we would never apply that kind of logic to any other realm of life and consider it normal.

"I'm a big coffee drinker, except I hate the way it smells, and especially the way it tastes."

"I love my family so much, but I'd rather spend time with anybody else but them."

"I've always been a huge, huge Mets fan. That's baseball, right?"

Ludicrous.

So even though we never exercise the nuclear "Gentile and tax collector" option until someone "refuses to listen to the church" for at least a year or more—or as long as there's any pulse or progress toward repentance—we do eventually reach the place where we must formally remove that person from the church rolls. We lament and weep and pray over this process and these people. We trust that God will continue to work in their lives, to woo them to faith. But for the ultimate good of their hearts and the protective good of the church, we must consider them unbelievers.

And it hurts. All the way around.

But wolves don't get to hang out with the sheep.

And broken fellowship was never meant to be any fun.

Redeeming Love

If you happen to be sheltering some bitterness in your heart—some resentment, some unforgiveness—and you just don't have a place to put it anymore . . .

If you're ducking to avoid people, trying hard to be wherever they're not, bucking the nudge of the Holy Spirit to go talk with this person, yet talking to anyone else who'll listen to your issues . . .

Or if you're increasingly sure that a friend or family member is giving in to some troubling behavior, and nobody seems willing to take the bull by the horns and ask the question . . .

The longer you put this off, the harder it's going to be. And the harder it gets, the less likely you'll be to do it. And if you're pretty sure you're never going to put yourself at risk of being the bad guy like that—even at the cost of a spoiled relationship, even at the potential cost of leaving someone to struggle all alone with their sin—then you're walking against the current of redemption. You're standing in the way of freedom, both yours and theirs. You're settling for what the gospel's done for *you*, without really caring what it can do for someone else.

What's a little loss of sleep if it could help you gain a brother?

Chapter 12

Pleasure Seekers

Persevering in the Pursuit of Joy

Sustainability is a word that has United Nations written all over it, maybe some kind of World Commission that advocates for soil conservation or forestry development or clean drinking water. And that's fine. Sounds responsible. As long as there's some Texas crude in there somewhere, we're all good.

But in thinking our way through the gospel, realizing that God roots it inside of people like us who are hardly the poster children for consistency, discipline, and long-range follow-through, how do we get it off the roundtable and into the field, out into the action? Beyond just assigning a task force and drawing up new lifestyle configurations and setting the alarm in the morning for 5:30—to start off on the right foot—why should we have any reason to believe we'll look up six weeks, six months, or six years from now and actually notice a difference?

How do we *sustain* it? How do we keep it going?

Most of us go in spurts. And realistically, we probably always will. The idea of nine-to-fiving our Christian faith, generating daily quotas of assembly-line output, invokes a kind of slide-rule expectation on our lives that doesn't really translate outside the engineering office. Just makes us more worried about reading those five or six extra Bible chapters before bed tonight—the ones we've gotten behind on in our reading plan—as opposed to snuggling with our kids and discovering what's on their heart.

So the problem that sustainability needs to fix is not the ebb and flow, the stop and start. We'll always have days that feel better and look better than others. What we're wanting to sustain is the snowballing of those small, regular, faith-infused moments that can build on each other, gain momentum, and propel us steadily ahead—what Nietzsche described (ironically, coming from him) as "a long obedience in the same direction."

But how do we do that? What keeps us rolling forward, even *falling* forward? In light of the finished work that God has already accomplished for us, how do we convert the spiritual nouns of justification, adoption, sanctification, vivification, mortification into something resembling a verb? And then a reverb? Until it's a sustained chord? A song? A symphony?

The simple answer—let's just get right to it here—is *joy*.

The *pursuit* of joy.

And in case that sounds just a little too esoteric for you, here's why it's actually not: *because you've been pursuing joy all your life.* All of us have. It's all we've ever done.

Everything you do in life stems from a desire to experience joy, pleasure, satisfaction, relief—you know, things from that word family. We are driven by the conviction, based on appetites living naturally inside the human heart, that certain actions will lead to happiness. People drink to pursue it. They have sex to pursue it. They go to the movies to pursue it. They play fantasy football to pursue it. They get married and have children to pursue it. They work sixty hours a week to pursue it. They go to the gym to pursue it. They go to church to pursue it. Oddly enough, in fact, people who went to church this week only because some pesky neighbor wouldn't get off their back about it—even though they'd have much rather stayed in bed and nibbled on pancakes and bacon with the Sunday paper—got up and went anyway . . . why? To pursue the even *more* desirable joy of getting their neighbor to maybe start leaving them alone about it.

Joy. We all want joy.

Everybody. All the time.

Now the two of us (both the pastor and the counselor) don't toss around words like *always* and *everything* without deliberate, careful intention. So when you hear us apply that kind of terminology in this case, you can bet we're doing it on purpose, not just being flippantly hyperbolic. So here you go: *Everything* you do is a joy pursuit. *Everything.* You do *nothing* that's not motivated by it.

And we're certainly not the first to see it that way. The seventeenth-century French mathematician and philosopher Blaise Pascal put it this way in his *Pensées* (meaning, "Thoughts") . . .

All men seek happiness. This is without exception. Whatever different means they employ, they all tend to this end. The cause of some going to war, and of others avoiding it, is the same desire in both, attended with different views. The will never takes the least step but

to this object. This is the motive of every action of every
man, even of those who hang themselves.[4]

Yes, "even those who hang themselves." And when you think
about it, you know it's true. Even in our desperation, even though
we absolutely know from experience and observation that the joy
or relief or escape we're seeking won't last (or *can't* last if we kill
ourselves, if it's the final time we ever seek it on earth), we still
never stop reaching for it. For joy.

Give us joy.

We'll do *anything* for it.

Then the gospel is the place for you. It's everything you've
been looking for. Because whether you want to believe this or not,
whether you'd accept it or not, whether it squares with what you've
always thought or not, the truth is this—and it's nearly the only
thing the Bible ultimately talks about: *man's greatest joy is in Jesus.*

Life with Him is better than anything else. Knowing Him
and being reconciled to the Father through Him is the one space
in which we find the most pleasurable, long lasting, irreplaceable
joy known to humanity.

You want examples? We've got examples.

There are many who say, "Who will show us some
good? Lift up the light of your face upon us, O Lord!"
You have put more joy in my heart than they have when
their grain and wine abound. (Ps. 4:6–7)

"Grain and wine" were symbols of wealth in the ancient
world. To have them in abundance was considered to be life's most
desirable and greatest attainment. The good life. And yet all these
many centuries later, housing projects and homeless shelters are

not the only places where you can occasionally hear sobbing on a Saturday night. Tears can fall and men can crumble, even in their book-lined studies in their gated communities or high overhead in their corporate jets. Women can collapse into a puddle of sorrow in a pair of pajamas that cost more than some of us spent on all of our Christmas gifts combined.

Are you pursuing joy by pursuing stuff and toys? Well . . . sorry, it's not there. It won't hold. The bricks will start sliding at some point. That tower of affluence and influence cannot keep you up above the pull of gravity unless the "joy in your heart" comes from somewhere much, much higher than that.

Only in God's "presence," David said, does "fullness of joy" linger and exist. "At your right hand are pleasures forevermore" (Ps. 16:11).

And speaking of great men in Bible history who reached this same, inescapable conclusion, we bring you the star of the New Testament as well (second only to the Lord Jesus, of course)—the apostle Paul, whose writings comprise up to half of that body of work.

Paul wasn't on the JV squad when it came to moral excellence, poise, and religious dedication. He was all-pro, all-world, and held records in all categories of first-century Jewish life: "circumcised on the eighth day, of the people of Israel, of the tribe of Benjamin, a Hebrew of Hebrews; as to the law, a Pharisee; as to zeal, a persecutor of the church; as to righteousness under the law, blameless" (Phil. 3:5–6).

Top that.

But as he paid it all forward, as he played out the string, as he stacked up all that good stuff into a monument to his own good name and reputation, it began to look less to him like a pile of unprecedented accomplishments and more like just a big pile of . . .

"Rubbish." You can thank the sensitive ears of the Bible translators for watching their language here, but this "rubbish" Paul was talking about—don't think of it as what you see at the garbage dump; think of it as what you see behind you in the toilet bowl. *There's* all your good works for you.

"Rubbish," he said. "Counted as loss," he said, when compared to the "surpassing worth of knowing Christ Jesus my Lord" (vv. 7–8).

If all our good-guy, good-girl churchgoing and choir singing and check writing and brownie baking don't serve their first and highest purpose by putting us more in love with Jesus, then, well . . . you know where you can stick it. Pardon our bluntness, we guess, but all that pretty stuff all by itself just really isn't worth much.

And yet for a lot of people, that's the track they're running on, the one they think is sure to lead them to joy eventually. But like everything else in life—including, of course, those things that look and sound a lot more sinful and selfish—it's not a road to depth and joy, but a life-sucking, joy-stealing treadmill.

Never gets them anywhere.

Because infinite joy comes only from Jesus.

"The thief comes only to steal and kill and destroy. I have come that they may have life, and have it to the full" (John 10:10 NIV).

The Greater Good

Seems to you, though, like all you're full of is sin. As hard as you try, your "long obedience" never seems to last much longer than a week or two. If anyone could ever accuse you of going in "the same direction" for a steady period of time, it would probably be down. Or nowhere. The old joke in AA meetings (not very funny, really) is that while everybody's inside fighting for victory over their addictions, their addictions are all outside in the parking lot doing pushups. Just waiting for them. *Feels* that way, at least.

So you work to keep it all confessed of, repented from. You line up a phalanx of blockers to help you fend off attack and hold you accountable. And since those people have other jobs to do and can't be out there watching over you every second (that's apparently what the NSA is for), then you stack up your defensive line of memory verses and drop back into zone coverage. Sounds like good thinking.

But why doesn't it always work very well?

Have you noticed? Why doesn't it sustain? Even with your game plan and strategy dialed up, you can sometimes be no more protected from being sacked for a loss than if you were out there all by yourself, you and whose army, you against the jailbreak of a safety blitz. How come?

Because we're hedonists, remember? We're pleasure seekers. Like a cell phone constantly searching for signal strength, we're always scanning for the things that'll give us the best shot at being happy. And temptation, by its very nature, is an appeal to our joy impulse. Although the promises that sin makes are promises it can't keep, they're often the kind of sweet promises we still love to hear.

Take *laziness*, for example. At the speeds which life demands us to travel anymore, a lot of those sighs and sweaty armpits out there in the work force are cues to start daydreaming about retirement or moving to the mountains, or about a job and family that don't ask or need so much of us, or about the memory of years gone by, when things seemed so much simpler and there was always time to kick back and cool our jets.

Could you find some joy in that?

But surprisingly, you'll find that lazy people are some of the most exhausted, complaining, dissatisfied, and ill-tempered folks around—because the joy-backed promises of laziness, at the roots, are lies that can't support their own arguments.

Sure, regular rhythms of rest and recharging are necessary, even *commanded* of us in Scripture (Ten Commandment #4) for keeping us healthy and balanced and happy in the Lord. But this notion that if we could somehow blow off our obligations for today, go spend the afternoon with our buddies, plop on the couch with a big bag of chips, some peanut M&Ms, and prime-time channel surfing till Letterman's over, and be assured of feeling absolutely wonderful by 11:30—that just very rarely works.

In fact—shattered paradigm warning here—the reality of life is that God intends us to be a little tired. Few things are more dangerous and disappointing than a bored man with too much time and energy on his hands. Read the Proverbs. See what comes from hard work, and compare it with what comes from taking your chances and hoping for a lucky break. Get the message. It's nothing you want.

Truth is, we're a lot better off, and a lot closer to experiencing real, feel-good moments, when we're wringing ourselves out for the glory of God and fulfilling our daily tasks—at work, at home, in ministry, anywhere. What did Vince Lombardi say in that famous speech: "I firmly believe that any man's finest hour—his greatest fulfillment to all he holds dear—is that moment when he has worked his heart out in a good cause and lies exhausted on the field of battle—victorious."[5]

Mmm. Man. You'll sleep good that night.

Satisfied exhaustion.

Because there's more joy in a job well done than in a job put off. Just is.

The sought-after pleasure of laziness is a lie. Same goes with *lust*. It promises soul-refreshing, mood-altering, permanent access to joy. Oh really? Wouldn't it feel just awesome to climb into bed at night after betraying your husband or wife? Wouldn't it feel great to abuse the weakened sensibilities of another man or woman? Don't you love fearing that the lady who just walked past you maybe saw you ogling her? Don't you feel totally invigorated and ready for the next day after scrolling through another page of porn shots on your computer before shutting down for the night?

No. You feel dirty, shameful, worthless, horrible, even angry.

Joyful? No, that was just for those fifteen, twenty, thirty minutes. And it better have been good. Good enough to outweigh this.

And yet it never is.

Or what about *anger*? Get mad enough, state your opinion loudly enough, voice your displeasure violently enough, and everybody's going to just completely come around to your way of thinking, right? You'll walk away feeling the pleasure of justice, of winning the argument, of getting your spouse to do what you want. Finally. Right?

Ha.

What you'll actually get back in return are relationships reduced to rubble, still vibrating from the aftershocks of your rage and unreasonableness—not justice. And not joy.

You want joy? Then work your tail off and put yourself in a position to look back and rejoice at what God has done through your responsible, diligent lifestyle. *You want joy?* Then invest every ounce of your romantic interests into the one who'll still be holding all your memories in her hand when you're seventy-five or eighty, and who'll still be wanting to hold *your* hand when you're out together as a couple. *You want joy?* Then wait on God's Spirit to work out your various conflicts and contentions, while He's also working on a few of the things in *you* that are bringing some of those very problems about—the way only He can, which is way better than whatever you're likely to work up by barging in with your own hammer and blueprints.

And so instead of using God's Word only as a weapon to try beating the bad stuff off of you, try using it instead as a gateway into joy—the *greater* joy of God's promises. Because as long as you're just out looking for joy anyway, why not look for it in the only place you can find it? Like, for example . . .

> Commit your work to the LORD, and your plans will be established. (Prov. 16:3)

> Blessed are the pure in heart, for they shall see God. (Matt. 5:8)

> Delight yourself in the LORD, and he will give you the desires of your heart. (Ps. 37:4)

How precious is your steadfast love, O God! The children of mankind take refuge in the shadow of your wings. They feast on the abundance of your house, and you give them drink from the river of your delights. For with you is the fountain of life; in your light do we see light. (Ps. 36:7–9)

You want joy? Then "set your minds on things that are above, not on things that are on earth. For you have died, and your life is hidden with Christ in God. When Christ who is your life appears, then you also will appear with him in glory" (Col. 3:1–4).

That's putting yourself on the offense.

That's letting joy drive out the imposters.

Sure, there are many good, defensive reminders in Scripture, things about making a "covenant" with your eyes not to look lustfully at another person (Job 31:1), about not letting "the sun go down on your anger" (Eph. 4:26), about being careful to pay close attention to wise counsel before you find yourself "at the brink of utter ruin in the assembled congregation" (Prov. 5:14). *Don't we need those?* Yes. They tell us the truth about the wickedness in our hearts. They reveal exactly who we are, if not for the redeeming mercy of Christ. And because of this reality, our battle will always include some saying no to things that are harmful to us and bring us pain.

But it will never be a *winning* battle, with a *sustainable* victory, if that's the only or primary way we try waging it. The anti-joy method. The grin-and-bear-it method. The suck-it-up method. The do-without-and-learn-to-like-it method.

Because we actually don't have to do without *anything*.

Our daily decisions not to participate in sin are only sacrifices if we're convinced those old friends of ours are sitting there holding our last, best chances for joy. But once we realize they've got *nothing* on us and on the sheer contentment that flows from walking with Jesus—contentment that's both full at the moment and yet constantly drawing us in for more—those soda cans of lame promises start tasting increasingly flat.

Let the world pursue whatever they want, thinking there's ultimate joy and pleasure waiting under that guillotine with the attractive, half-naked woman beside it, asking you to lay your head down *r-i-g-h-t* here, right on this nice little stump. Put gobs of money on top of it. Park a new car behind it. Stand some important business contacts around it, or anything that's often felt to you like it would be the greatest thing possible if you could have it.

And let everybody knock themselves out going for it.

Because when all those allures have packed up and gone home, and their victims look back on a life spent chasing those joy-baiters with all their might, the only things left will be blood and horror and another tragic testimony to tell their children and grandchildren, of the "thousand" and "ten thousand" who've fallen to the same, sorry fate (Ps. 91:7).

But you know what? Those cheap versions of joy don't ever need to come "near you," not again, like that verse from Psalm 91 goes on to say—because you've found the one-and-only joy in life, the joy that comes from being at home in Jesus.

Treasure Hunters

He once told a quick, one-paragraph parable (Matt. 13:44) about a man who came across a treasure hidden in a field. Don't know what the guy was looking for. Don't know what he'd considered to be his dream pursuit and discovery up until that time. But when his shovel struck whatever was holding the secret of this indescribable treasure, he covered it back up, took immediate action to liquidate his assets, and used the money he made from the sale to purchase that whole field, to own that treasure.

To experience ultimate joy.

An unseen kingdom occupies the same spaces where we interact with daily life. It's underground, it's in the air. It defies the structures of physics and chemistry. But as people whom God has drawn toward the truth and promises of the gospel, we have been given the vision through Christ to recognize this kingdom when we see it, as well as the hand tools to dig into it and open it up.

We've been given the Holy Spirit to awaken our deadened hearts, turning our glaring, gravitational limitations into opportunities for visiting heavenly places. That's a joy.

We've been given His holy Word, revealing to us more truth about ourselves than we ever imagined would be exposed—things that *we* didn't even know—and yet surrounding our brokenness with His personal knowledge and care for us, with His all-sufficient presence and love. With joy.

We've been given a platform for communicating with Him, not through layers of red tape or fifteen-minute appointments that won't be coming available for at least six months, but rather the freedom of talking with Him instantly, as quickly as we can think it. It's just another reason to be joyful.

All the spiritual disciplines and means of grace that allow us to live in this kingdom, with anytime access to our Father God, have been opened for us to enter and experience who our Creator really is, to worship Him with our whole hearts, and to know a life that transcends the most euphoric achievements and enjoyments of human potential.

If the greatest tragedy of Eden was the loss of intimate fellowship with the Maker of our souls, the greatest joy of life in His kingdom is the restoration of this intimacy we lost.

And why should we expect anything else to rival this pleasure? Why would any other suitor seem a worthy competitor? Why would anyone fashioned as a hedonist—like we are—from the creation of the world, not want to be the most unabashed, undaunted, uninhibited seeker of pleasure that he or she could possibly be? Why be "half-hearted creatures," as C. S. Lewis wrote in *The Weight of Glory*, "fooling about with drink and sex and ambition when infinite joy is offered us, like an ignorant child who wants to go on making mud pies in a slum because he cannot imagine what is meant by the offer of a holiday at sea. We are far too easily pleased."[6]

Oh, let this not be said of us. Let's be the kind of people who, upon finding the treasure chest, tear back toward our homes and everyday lives, shake down the house, taking every unnecessary, underperforming piece of property from the rooms and walls and closets and baseboards, and cashing every bit of it in for the treasure He's shown us within the kingdom He's prepared for us.

You don't need to quell the hedonistic desire that leads you into sin and selfishness; you just need to redirect it into places where that desire can finally hit the target.

And when it does, you'll want to stay there for a long, long time.

Epilogue

Making Much of His Name

So . . . that's our cover version of the gospel.

It began amid the glories and freedom and fullness of the Garden, in complete unity of heart and mind with our Creator. Then our connection to Him was rocked off its hinges by the slithering intrusion of sin into the human habitat.

And it broke us. Beyond self-repair. There was no ladder high enough, and no wall to lean it against anyway. Completely lost, completely helpless, death without parole.

Except . . .

The Creator refused to abandon His creation. And though our preference would've been to fix the problem ourselves, without needing His help, without admitting our inability, He pursued us in our foolishness. And through the just but sacrificial offering of His unblemished and holy Son, He redeemed His fallen people for Himself by the wise, loving pleasure of His eternal will.

For our established guilt—*justification*.

And for our debilitating shame—*adoption*.

We're given innocence. Pardoned.

We're made His children. To be delighted in.

No fear. No anxiety. Simply peace and prosperity.

And by virtue of these indescribable gifts, consummated by the entry of the Holy Spirit into our lives, we are now equipped by His indwelling power to sanctify our still-rebellious wants and desires until we increasingly, progressively grow up into the image of our Savior Christ.

Our separation from God is ended.

Forever.

We are His.

We are saved.

But as He continues His recovery efforts on these stubborn pockets of resistance that still exist in our hearts, He invites us to initiate simultaneously the recovery of relationships that have been torn and damaged by a combination of the Fall and the unleashing of our own deliberate sins. Our reconnection with God, so unquestionably strong and secure, means we can now reach toward others without needing the acceptance and approval we've already received from the Lord, but rather with the freedom to pour out into their lives the forgiveness and peace of Christ.

And though we wake up every morning on a fractured planet, and though pieces of our brokenness still flake off every day, we have found in Christ a joy beyond all other joys, and we are prepared by His boundless grace to persevere to the very end . . . till our faith becomes sight, till we see Him face to face.

Till we are completely changed.

God be praised.

So with this story as prologue, with these promises in force, we are released from mankind's obsession with self and protection and brand recognition. We can just roll out of bed tomorrow with the one-note ambition of making much of His name. Instead of getting off-track with our various attempts at redemption, instead of bogging down in guilt and shame, in fear and anxiety, everyday life becomes simply an ongoing opportunity for worship. Not in some weird, artificial, singsong way. Instead, we let every action, enjoyment, work detail, and relational experience—even the hard and challenging stuff—roll up into thanksgiving toward Him for all He has done for us and the song He's continually teaching us to sing.

That's why Jesus declared us to be the "light of the world . . . a city set on a hill" (Matt. 5:14), because only a gross misunderstanding or diminution of the gospel would make us want to keep His glory "hidden" within us, to have this flame of His presence blazing inside and yet to fearfully "put it under a basket" (v. 15). Left to ourselves and the strength of our volunteerism, we can only show the restricted reach of a man or woman's possibilities. But when backed by the redemptive working of Almighty God, all the resurrection power of Christ is available for display through us.

And we're fools not to want to get in on that.

Redemption that's been received but not recovered can result in several different kinds of dysfunction:

Spiritual anemia, where we limit the amount of wisdom, mercy, and service we can pour out on others because we haven't been taking in an ample amount of nourishment ourselves from the Word, from fellowship with other believers, from time spent loving and worshipping and stirring up our affections for Jesus.

Spiritual bulimia, where we've put ourselves in places to hear the Word and be filled with the Lord's presence, and yet we don't digest it, we don't savor it, we don't walk away changed by it. As soon as we're back in our comfortable places, away from God's people, we throw it all up and gorge ourselves on something else.

Spiritual obesity, where we love scooting up to the table, love the taste and flavor of Christian food, love to eat and eat and eat some more, but basically grow constipated on it without ever working it out into muscle mass and physical action. It's like puffing into a balloon until our face turns red and our eyes bug out . . . till eventually, it pops.

It can happen.

If you've suffered from one of these, you *know* they can happen. And you know how sick they can make you feel.

So as you begin to process the grand implications of such a great salvation, we call you out of dysfunction and into mission with the risen Lord—not necessarily to Africa or Mongolia, but also not within the artificial boundaries of a backed-off, backed-down, change-averse spiritual mentality. Where you've cordoned yourself off from what you consider to be the dangerous fringes of the general population, it's time now to believe enough in the power of the gospel that you'll launch yourself into any situation God leads you toward, confident that He can use you to accomplish some eternal things with Him—not because *you're* there, but because *He's* there. *In* you.

One thing we should all be clear on by now is that Christians are as goofed up and naturally flawed as every person who'll drive down your street today. God's grace is the only intervening factor that's changed any of that. And so whatever sense of superiority that's possibly slipped into your head, you can be sure it's all coming from you, not from what the gospel and God's Word is telling you. So when you frame up walls around your house and around your family to keep the world from coming in, to make certain you stay purer than you actually are, the monster you're closing in is no better than the one you're locking out. Obviously, of course, we need to apply some wisdom here—with our kids especially—not recklessly sailing them into situations they're not age-appropriately ready to handle. But some of us are so afraid we're going to be infected by the sin virus, we refuse to look people's needs in the eye and realize their sickness is no worse than ours, at least no worse than ours *was*, and no worse than it would *still* be if God's grace didn't have us covered.

The recovery of your redemption means you need to run downstairs right now and be sure the front door to your house—and more importantly, the front and back doors of your heart—are still functionally able to swing into a fully opened position. And that's how they need to stay. Propped open.

Your neighbors ought to know there's more that's happened to you than just whatever makes your car not be in the driveway on Sunday morning. They ought to be so confused by the care and thoughtfulness and openness and genuine believability you exhibit on a routine basis, they don't really know what to make of you. The people where you work—where God has divinely placed your body and your skill set—shouldn't be left to wonder that you care deeply about what matters to them, not only by the compassion and interest you show them, but by the integrity and honor and diligence that reflects the nature of the One who actually signs your paycheck.

But while not overlooking the personal, one-on-one nature of this gospel difference in your life, be sure not to restrict the change it evokes in you to thank-you notes and birthday cards and kind offers to rake the leaves in someone's yard. As people who've been rescued from our own very realistic sense of helplessness, despair, and poverty, this same open door should extend beyond the boundaries of nearby convenience to include a heart for the needy and neglected, the undervalued and disenfranchised.

There's no guidebook that tells you exactly what this needs to look like or what it needs to involve. There's simply a commission: "Go therefore and make disciples of all nations, baptizing them in the name of the Father and of the Son and of the Holy Spirit, teaching them to observe all that I have commanded you" (Matt. 28:19–20). God is faithful enough to put this challenge into motion for you and direct you toward the places where you can uniquely plug in your gospel light.

But don't go off trying to do something, thinking God won't be proud of you till you do. And don't feel pressure to follow up on it just to prove something to other people, to be involved in the kind of measurable ministries you'll be able to put on your Christmas letter. If you're receiving this challenge as guilt or a burden, you're not understanding us.

Gospel-motivated worship leads to gospel-empowered ministry and mission. Being gospel-centered and saturated leads to a joy-filled submission toward all that He calls to do, based on all we've been given. Making much of His name means living freely within His grace-based provision, not angling to get something He's already given you.

So whatever activities and interests fill up the 120 hours or so each week when you're not sleeping off the other fifty or sixty, they now can all be attached in some way to the gospel you've received. *All* of them.

Investing in your marriage.

Living in shared fellowship with other believers.

Wrestling with your kids in the backyard.

Viewing your work as a daily offering of thanks.

Stopping to listen, even if it costs you an errand.

Celebrating each meal as proof of His provision.

Praying in between your appointments.

Thanking Him for every blessing . . .

. . . and for that one . . .

. . . and that one . . .

Loving Him. Just loving Him.

And enjoying being loved.

Letting your light shine.

Pushing back the darkness.

Not just *being* redeemed.

Living redeemed.

Changed.

Acknowledgments

From Matt:

This is my fourth project and I have learned that putting a book together is very much a team effort. I'd like to thank the elders of The Village Church for giving me time to study, prepare and write. Serving alongside you in the great cause is one of the gifts God has graciously given me. To the staff members at The Village who labored behind the scenes to make this project a reality—I am thankful for your tireless, gospel-centered ministry to me and the church. Michael Snetzer, your ability and willingness to counsel people with the Word of God is as convicting as it is encouraging. I will never forget sitting at El Chico and dreaming about how to help the most broken among us. Lawrence Kimbrough has been a real gift to us, taking our scattered thoughts, writings, manuscripts and teaching outlines and creating something readable and helpful. No one would be holding this project in their hands without your hard work—thank you! Finally, I would like to acknowledge my wife, Lauren. No one bears the brunt of my mind being on a project like you do. Thanks for being such a sounding board, encourager and general editor of everything in my life. I love you!

From Michael:

I give thanks to the collaboration of the original Artist from which this cover comes. You are the greatest Songwriter the world has ever known and the depths of your creative genius are unsearchable. I am grateful to B&H Publishing for their partnership in this project. In particular I want to thank Lawrence Kimbrough. Lawrence, you are an extraordinary gift and I am grateful to call you friend. Thank you for all your hard work in making this book a reality. I also want to acknowledge John Henderson, who among so many other blessings in my life suggested the title of this work.

I am grateful for all the pastors (not the least of whom is Matt), teachers, mentors, supervisors and counselors who influenced and trained me in the gospel and its application. I want to acknowledge all those who have gone before me and laid down their lives that I might know Jesus and the power of His resurrection. I am especially grateful for my co-laborers in Christ, particularly at The Village Church, without whom (through the power of the Holy Spirit) I would not have seen the manifold wisdom of God on display among us in such powerful ways. Finally, I must acknowledge and thank my beautiful wife Sonia and all that she sacrifices so that I might do this work. Sonia, thank you for your faithfulness and tenacious love for our children.

Notes

1. We've borrowed and adapted the following structure from Thomas Watson, a seventeenth-century Puritan, whose *The Doctrine of Repentance* does as good a job as any of laying out what "godly grief" looks like. We would've asked his permission first, but didn't think he'd mind. Actually, we think it'd *blow* his mind to know his little pamphlet from the 1600s is now in public domain all across a Web-connected world. Hope you'll go look it up yourself. Good reading.

2. You can find a lengthier explanation of this concept from Ezekiel 14 in Paul David's Tripp's *Instruments in the Redeemer's Hands* (Phillipsburg, NJ: P&R Publishing, 2002).

3. Some of the concepts we present in this chapter are inspired by Ken Sande's *The Peacemaker* (Grand Rapids, MI: Baker Books, 2004). Can't commend this resource to you highly enough. Get it and read it.

4. Pascal quote is from Pensées, see http://www.ccel.org/ccel/pascal/pensees.pdf.

5. "What It Takes to Be Number One," http://www.vincelombardi.com/number-one.html.

6. C. S. Lewis, *The Weight of Glory* (New York: MacMillan, 1980).

WHAT'S NEXT?

We drift from the gospel and our reorientation to the gospel is a life-long process. Real transformation happens best in the context of biblical community.

Explore in depth the truths taught in Recovering Redemption with this video-driven 12-week Bible study featuring video teaching from Matt Chandler.

www.recoveringredemption.com